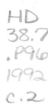

Protecting Corporate America's Secrets in the Global Economy

A Risk Analysis of the New Threats to U.S. Business Information

AIBR
American Institute for Business Research

Published by
American Institute for Business Research
in cooperation
with the
National Security Institute

This publication is designed to provide accurate and authoritative information in regard to the subject matter covered. It is sold with the understanding that the publisher is not engaged in rendering legal, accounting, or other professional service. If legal advice or other expert assistance is required, the services of a competent professional should be sought. *From a Declaration of Principles jointly adopted by a Committee of the American Bar Association and a Committee of Publishers.*

Copyright © 1992
American Institute for Business Research, Inc.
161 Worcester Road
Framingham, Massachusetts 01701
(508) 820-3424

Library of Congress Catalog Card Number
92-72907

ISBN 0-9633534-0-3

Printed in the United States of America

Table of Contents

Executive Summary

"There is going to be far more espionage, but it's going to be economic, financial espionage. Knowledge is strategic intelligence. Corporations are going to be hotbeds of spies. They will be reporting back to governments, and the fusion of private intelligence and public is inevitable."

— *Alvin Toffler in USA Today interview on his book "Powershift"*

T he global competitiveness of U.S. corporations is under siege by a diverse group of professional information gatherers whose mission is to acquire proprietary information. The attackers include disgruntled employees from the inside and electronic eavesdroppers from the outside.

Senior managers at many major U.S. multinational corporations have failed to take these risks seriously, according to many security experts, and are thus unwittingly losing billions of dollars per year. Those managers who have taken the threat seriously are now finding that the laws are inadequate to protect them.

Perhaps the most considerable threat comes from foreign intelligence operators — sponsored by both friendly and hostile governments — who have begun to target sensitive corporate information that can be turned to economic advantage.

Glasnost may have occasioned a thaw in East-West relations, but many of the spies who have come in from the cold are as busy as ever. Instead of spying on each other, however, foreign intelligence agencies are focusing on industrial espionage, with U.S. technology as one of the prime targets, according to many security experts who warn that much of that data lies unprotected.

Instead of the latest weapons design or secret arms specifications, the spies of the 1990s prefer the secrets of AT&T Bell Laboratories' fiber optics communications, General Motors' ceramic engine designs, IBM's computer technology and Quaker Oats' techniques in processing and packaging their goods.

"Industrial espionage is highly profitable," according to a former director of Soviet KGB covert activities in the Far East who defected to the U.S. in 1979. He adds that Russia, increasingly strapped for hard currency as well as technology, will boost its industrial espionage efforts "manyfold from what it was a few years ago."

Former foes are not the only worry, however. Longtime allies are also prying into U.S. technological interests. For example, in November, 1990, W. Douglas Gow, a Federal Bureau of Investigation assistant director who heads Foreign Counterintelligence Operations, confirmed reports in a television interview that France's General Director of Exterior Security tried to hire employees in the European offices of IBM, Texas Instruments, Inc. and other U.S. electronics companies to provide information for pay.

As more U.S. corporations expand their businesses worldwide, the problem of information theft by professional snoops will likely worsen, security experts say. The awareness of this potential risk is alarmingly low, they add.

Tactics employed in the new espionage are the same as those used in the traditional game of spy vs. spy. The methods include such traditional techniques as planting agents within American corporations who pass trade secrets to foreign intelligence services, who in turn pass them to foreign competitors. There have also been cases where agents did not steal information but served as "influence agents" — corporate executives who can affect high-level corporate decision-making in ways favorable to foreign governments or competitors.

Other methods include the widespread use of electronic listening devices — bugging hotel rooms, residences and even commercial airline seats. There have also been cases where foreign governments have searched the trash of American corporate executives looking for trade secrets. Front companies have also been set up for economic espionage purposes, as a means of providing greater access to facilities and personnel with valuable proprietary information.

What can U.S. firms do to protect themselves from industrial espionage? Most experts say the single greatest mistake managers make is failing to take the threat seriously.

Few companies are even aware that this sort of electronic eavesdropping is going on and are skeptical when alerted to possible security breaches, says Thomas Sobczak, vice president of Application Configured Computers, Inc., a security consulting and software publishing company in Baldwin, N.Y. The company also maintains a database of classified and sensitive information that has leaked out of federal agencies and large corporations.

The debate over how to "level the playing field" of international competitiveness in response to economic espionage has two sides. There are those who say that because the French, Japanese, Russians and others are targeting U.S. firms, American intelligence must respond in kind.

Some in Congress say the Central Intelligence Agency and the National Security Agency should match the industrial intelligence-gathering activities of U.S. allies such as France, Britain and Japan, which have traditionally shared intelligence data with industry. For example, in the hearings on the nomination of Robert Gates to head the CIA, Gates came under pressure to commit to a similar linkage with American industry.

What really counts in terms of economic competitiveness is not secret information, but using material available from open sources with sound business judgment that will make a difference in the world marketplace. Ninety-nine percent of what is needed to be competitive as a nation can be learned on the playing fields of free markets and through free exchanges, information that has very little to do with the world of intelligence.

An increasing number of companies have come to realize that much of what they need to know about their competitors can be gathered by "information agents" who are the vanguard of a still-emerging corporate enterprise called competitive intelligence (CI).

Any collection of information about a competitor, just a decade ago, was dismissed with a sneer as spying, something that exists on the same moral plane as peeking into your neighbor's mailbox. Corporate America, seeing the advantages it gave its overseas competitors and hearing the admonitions from academia, have embraced the concept at an accelerating pace.

Every company, no matter how careful, leaves information behind in the same way that a battleship leaves a wake or a submarine a sound signature

---

If corporate intelligence really were espionage it might be a lot simpler to combat. However, since the lion's share of the work is building pictures from disparate bits of information by inference and extrapolation, it's nearly impossible to totally stop. Every company, no matter how careful, leaves information behind in the same way that a battleship leaves a wake or a submarine a sound signature.

Companies as diverse as McDonnell Douglas, Helene Curtis, AT&T, Xerox, Kodak, Digital Equipment Corp., Coors Brewing, NutraSweet and Corning have invested directly in developing their CI-functional departments.

Smaller companies, although they may not have the resources to staff full-time CI units, have identified CI's role and assigned the CI function to existing personnel. One expert contends that smaller companies are often better practitioners of CI than the giants. He says they know what they want, know what to do once they get it and the essence of the information collected is not lost from filtering it through layers of bureaucracy.

Most all of the aggressive digging by CI agents can be counteracted in the corporate environment by instituting a single command: Thou shalt not speak to strangers. "Strangers" in this context refers to callers whose identity has yet to be verified. No company would want to allow unauthorized persons to have access to the computers where its information is stored. This same rule should apply to the most dynamic storage agents: the company's employees.

Every employee has the potential to harm his employer by injudicious disclosure, but there are certain key corporate employees that all CI professionals relish capturing on the phone for an interview. Among the functionaries that companies should warn about giving away the family jewels are personnel in marketing, sales, public relations/investor relations, corporate librarians and purchasing agents.

Security experts advise that all employees be screened carefully, and previous employment references prodded for all information about the candidates, and employees' careers. Any "holes" in the resume should be immediate cause for suspicion and for vigorous investigation. That period of missing time on the resume could be the interval during which that employee candidate was working for a competitor — and maybe still is. New hires should be required to read and sign a binding confidentiality agreement.

As well, security experts advise, employees leaving a company should be completely debriefed, reminded of their confidentiality agreement and called to account for all records and computer files in their possession during their term of employment.

Computer systems — the technology used to house information — are increasingly coming under attack in a variety of ways, ranging from outlaw hackers who tamper with systems for fun to professional snoops intent on prying loose company secrets.

Using any information technology, as a matter of course, incurs its own particular risk. The fax, cellular phone, inter-plant microwave link — who could do business without these information vehicles? These days, very few companies. Who then, can disregard how these technologies of convenience may be tools for the intruder as well as for the user? No one. Never before has doing business been so convenient, yet never before have corporate spies had the opportunities that they have now.

Corporate America is rushing to "downsize" their computer applications from large mainframe computers to local area networks (LANs) that often link hundreds, and even thousands, of personal computers. At the same time companies may be installing "client/server" architectures, which transfer some computer processing from mainframes to PCs and other computers connected to LANs.

"From a security standpoint, multi-vendor connectivity is a nightmare," says Daniel White, partner and national director of Information Security at Ernst & Young in Chicago. "PC security is still an oxymoron."

As a result, connecting personal computers and other types of computers (usually made by a variety of different manufacturers) has become one of the most pressing security issues facing systems administrators and security managers. Many existing systems have older technologies that do not embrace security features, strong access controls, or audit trails. They were designed with performance, not security, in mind. Even today, security considerations must wrestle with the perennial objection that security routines inhibit access by users.

Companies with a mobile sales or maintenance force or a large contingent of outside contractors also must have a system open enough for their employees to use no matter where they are, including in their homes and on the road.

The portable office is still a relatively new concept with high security vulnerability because it involves remote access and radio links. The office can now span the globe, be extended into any den or kitchen in the world, places that might not have the same information security level as the office.

Some people now use portable PCs from their hotel rooms or even hook PCs and faxes up to cellular radios, easy targets for eavesdropping. Every keystroke, including passwords and access codes that are transmitted over a system is available to anyone who wishes to intercept that communication.

If the corporate spy would name one darling of his trade it would have to be the modern, full-featured fax. It's convenient; one has to monitor the line; and once it is tapped, the information thief need only turn on his fax. When the target's fax transmission is activated, the thief's fax will dutifully turn out its own copy of the materials being sent or received. Though that is not the extent of the fax's vulnerability to espionage.

The rapid adoption of distributed computer systems, electronic data interchange (EDI), local-area networks and other technology has outpaced the capacity of most companies to secure them against attack.

Telecommunications networks, especially those that cross international boundaries, are also more vulnerable to electronic industrial espionage.

Networks of all types, not just for computers, have proliferated out of control, creating security problems and augmenting the number of potential points of unauthorized entry into company computer systems. The networks are without end points, and most information systems (IS) managers do not even know how extensive their networks really are.

The information technologies like Telex that make business faster, easier and more convenient than ever before have opened up entirely new vectors of vulnerability for businesses, creating inviting routes of penetration for corporate spies.

Many corporate communications networks are poorly designed for security. The primary criteria for selecting networks too often addresses finding the lowest cost solution. The guiding principles of network design, however, are wide connectivity, universal access for company personnel and ease of maintenance for network managers. Companies will pay money for those features but security is most often considered a separate issue, something to be considered after purchasing systems and service contracts.

The demand for corporate telecommunications services is rapidly increasing with companies offering electronic data interchange, information storage, and electronic mail. Companies very often are outsourcing their entire telecommunications operation to a third party company that will provide hardware, maintenance and staffing. In virtually none of the cases is security and increased vulnerability of these services considered.

The trend in telecommunications requirements is toward faster and lower cost long-haul service and access to more (and bigger) databases by more people in scattered geographic locations. For reasons of perception, though, usually it is the computer systems that get the benefit of a security envelope.

When companies contract for private telecommunication networks, invariably, keeping costs low is a major factor and little or no thought is given to the protection of the information against corporate wiretappers. This practice flies in the face of technical realities and recent history. The first international computer privateers were by necessity "phone phreaks" versed in the mechanics of busting into central offices. As deregulation takes information on communications technologies further from the hands of the AT&T priesthood, the distribution of knowledge on how to crack phone systems can only increase.

Corporate networks offer tappers faster returns than public switched networks; they are far easier to wiretap for voice communications or rig for computer data interception. It is primarily dedicated to the function of the corporation, which means information on the network is not mixed in with non-corporate information. This allows a single penetration to accrue maximum data interception. This centralization also reduces the amount of work an infiltrator must perform to tap into the right phone lines.

Instead of, say, hiring a proxy to sift through lines at a Bell Company's central offices, calling back and trying to fool the company's employees into confirming the phone numbers of the lines they are tapping, a tapper who manages to break into, say, a PBX has already done all the searching he needs.

Interception of corporate communication systems is possible with high quality, off-the-shelf hardware that 10 years ago existed only in the professional intelligence services of the world, but now is available to anyone, including competitors, hackers and free-lance information thieves. Combatting these privateers is less a work of inspiration in the heat of battle and more a thoughtful preparation for long-term siege.

Major corporations will also have to contend with attacks on their computer systems, data centers and networks by terrorists, special-interest groups and politically-minded hackers.

Attacks on computer systems already account for some 60% of all terrorist attacks in the world, says Martin Cetron, president of Forecasting International Ltd., a consulting firm based in Arlington, Va. In an article published in *The Futurist* magazine in 1989, Cetron said 24 computer centers were bombed in West Germany in one year. Italy's Red Brigades and France's *Action Directe* have also targeted computer systems in Europe. "It is only a matter of time before someone takes advantage of U.S. computer vulnerability," he says.

Security is frequently considered tedious and the costs of implementing and managing a security program seem greater than the risks, but the consequences of fraud can be crippling. According to experts over 90 percent of the companies that depend on electronic systems and experience a serious disruption of their data processing operations go out of business.

There are several ways for a company to protect its computer system against intrusion, ranging from setting up audit trails to physically isolating the computer system and limiting access to it. But there is no single solution; nearly all information managers know that it takes a combination of methods to create a fail-safe system.

Experts say that many security breaches succeed because the obvious physical security procedures have been overlooked and not from the result of sophisticated electronic theft.

Taking such precautions as locking doors, restricting access to personal computers and workstations and properly disposing of materials that may provide clues to the inner workings of a company's computer operations is an effective first line of defense, the experts say.

Devices such as "tokens" and "smart cards," which are designed to generate new passwords for computer access every time they are used, are slowly becoming popular as alternatives to traditional password management methods.

Biometric security devices examine the physical actions or traits that make each individual unique. They work in a similar manner: A biometric portrait of the subject is scanned or read by sensor devices, converted into digital data and stored. In verification, the subject's handprint, voice or other trait is compared with the stored profile.

Cryptographic methods can be used to protect not only the confidentiality of data, but the integrity of data as well. Data confidentiality is the protection of information from unauthorized disclosure. Data integrity is the protection of information from unauthorized modification.

Cryptography of computer data is also being revolutionized by so-called public key cryptographic systems — considered the strongest yet by many industry analysts. In public key cryptographic systems, the user publishes his "public key" and correspondents use it to encrypt messages to the user. The only key that can decrypt the message is the user's "secret key."

All the hardware and cryptography in the world, however, no matter how elegantly assembled, can't ensure a totally secure environment

---

In this way, the public key method provides encryption and authentication of the receiver's identity. From a security standpoint, if correctly implemented, a significant improvement in security is provided. Like any system, however, the specific applications and implementation are extremely important.

Communications security technologies are available in as many different price ranges and choices as there are for, say, electronic testing equipment. In larger corporations, because of the complexity of today's information networks and the growing multitude of protection options, employing a skilled security architect is virtually a necessity for an effective solution at lowest cost. Containing costs is always easier for someone who knows the market, knows the problem, and can pick the appropriate, lowest-cost solutions.

The good news is even the most advanced protection is rapidly coming down in price. Currently, government agencies and U.S. defense contractors are using a secure communications telephone handset called the STU-III which can encrypt voice or data communications. The STU-III was developed by the National

Security Agency (NSA) and is selling for around $2000 — a considerable discount from the STU-II it replaced. As yet there is no published plan for the U.S. intelligence community to make the instrument available on the commercial market. There are, however, a growing array of commercial products that provide secure telephonic communications, presumably less effective than the STU-III but powerful nonetheless.

All the hardware and cryptography in the world, however, no matter how elegantly assembled, can't ensure a totally secure environment without the intelligent participation of personnel and the integration of security regimes into the workaday cadence of the office or manufacturing environment.

Data security does not have to be an all or nothing proposition. Analysts suggest that for a typical company only about 5% to 10% of the data needs to be protected. In fact, protecting up to 80% of company data would use up only 20% of a security budget; it is the final 20% of data that would be most costly to protect, the experts say.

For a typical company different levels of security may be used to protect proprietary information. The highest level of security should be provided to mission critical and extremely sensitive information such as strategic plans, trade secrets, etc. A medium level of security is recommended for sensitive information, such as company finances and product plans. A lower level of security considerations should be accorded to such information as the payroll, personnel files, medical records, etc.

Private companies should follow the example of the government in classifying documents, several security experts contend. Doing so could be key to convincing a court of sincerity and dedication in protecting trade secrets in the event of a security breach and may help prevent such problems in the first place.

A company's secrets consist not of national security information but of proprietary technical data and confidential business information; however, they can be appraised in a similar way to those of government by determining which items could benefit competitors and cause potential harm to the company if they became known to others. Consultants suggest that documents judged to contain secrets should be labeled as such. They also suggest that documents be regularly declassified, since a company's laxness in this respect could leave courts unimpressed about its claims of confidentiality and of violations thereof: if everything is classified, nothing is special.

Some consultants recommend business practices that parallel the U.S. government's security clearance process. It is sometimes recommended that employers compile a list of trade secrets which a prospective employee might have access to and then assess the potential damage to the company in the event of their collective or individual loss.

Employees should be evaluated for their trustworthiness during job interviews in light of such potential damage they could cause the company. Most companies cannot carry out the extensive background checks that federal agencies sometimes perform, but it is often prudent to assign or hire an investigator to verify data supplied by the job applicant.

One difference between business and government is the former's greater reliance on employee agreements. Explicit discussion with employees of the risks surrounding trade secrets and their signing of contracts that set out what they can and cannot do with information they learn while working for a company are key elements in impressing a court with the seriousness of an information-protection program.

Knowledge today, arguably, is the greatest corporate asset. At no time in history has the value of information been at such a premium. Yet, the information keepers of the corporate kingdom are letting the treasures of the crown slip away in the dark of night and in the shadows of intrigue while they dig bigger and better moats and higher and higher walls.

Chapter 1:

U.S. Companies are Prime Targets of Economic Espionage

"Once preoccupied with penetrating intelligence services and other government agencies, and obtaining political and military secrets, the spies of the 1990s are targeting American corporations for the trade secrets and proprietary information that has been at the root of and key to United States economic power."

— *William S. Sessions Director, Federal Bureau of Investigation*

A s the Cold War wanes, foreign intelligence services — both friendly and hostile to the United States — that once focused exclusively on military and geopolitical competition and conflict are now busily shifting their efforts to the economic arena. Intelligence and military information is still being sought, but the targets now also include the secrets of corporate boardrooms and research laboratories.

Instead of the latest weapons design or secret arms specifications, the spies of the 1990s prefer the secrets of AT&T Bell Laboratories' fiber optics communications, General Motors' ceramic engine designs, IBM's computer technology and Quaker Oats' techniques in processing and packaging their goods.

"Direct theft of American private sector secrets by foreign government intelligence services is not yet a massive undertaking," notes Senator David Boren, (D-Okla.), outgoing Chairman of the Senate Intelligence Committee, "but as we go into the next century, and as international relations become much more a matter of economic competition than military competition . . . it's going to really increase."

As FBI Intelligence Division Chief Thomas DuHadway put it in August 1991: "Economic information is highly sought after because it translates back into economic power, and that's the name of the game in this day and age."

Former Foes, Former Friends

The new security threat environment can be traced to two signal events. The collapse of the Berlin Wall in November 1989 and the failed coup in the Kremlin in August 1991. Both marked historic turning points in the area of international counterintelligence and security. The rapid reunification of Germany that followed led to the abrupt disbanding of East Germany's vast security and foreign intelligence apparatus. Although many of the East German intelligence agents were transferred to Soviet control, for all practical purposes the East German intelligence service ceased to exist.

In Poland, Czechoslovakia, and Hungary democratic governments emerged which viewed the political police of the past communist regimes as instruments of oppression at home and surrogates for the Soviet KGB abroad. Today, according to the FBI, the East German, Polish, Czech and Hungarian intelligence services and their activities in the United States are out of business. In fact, some of these former communist states are now cooperating with U.S. counterintelligence in uncovering Americans who spied for the other side. The Romanian and Bulgarian intelligence services continue to spy, although not at the same levels as before.

For corporate security generally, the passing of the East German HVA intelligence service was highly significant. The HVA, with renowned German efficiency, developed a reputation over the past four decades as one of the most aggressive and successful collectors of high-technology information from both government and private American corporations.

The announced disbanding of the KGB following the events of August 1991, on the other hand, has had only a limited impact on the largest foreign intelligence service in the world. The former KGB global intelligence collection and active measures infrastructure remains intact and continues, at least at the present time, to pose a formidable threat to U.S. security.

Asked if the former KGB, now the Russian Foreign Intelligence Agency, has given up hostile activities against the United States, FBI Director William Sessions presented some not-so-surprising news: The former KGB, although no longer the "state-within-a-state" it once was, is continuing its intelligence-gathering against the West under the reformist Russian government of Boris Yeltsin. The new Russian foreign intelligence chief, Yevgeni Primakov, a former key player in the Soviet Communist Party's disinformation apparatus, says that foreign spying will shift to economic targets, in order to support the new non-communist economy. "Of course, one of our emphases will shift to the commercial sphere, that's quite natural," Primakov says, adding that "critical technologies" will be one of the new targets of spying.

Director Sessions says foreign intelligence services in the post-Cold War era are shifting the focus of the collection priorities. Once preoccupied with penetrating intelligence services and other government agencies, and obtaining political and military secrets, the spies of the 1990s are targeting American corporations for the trade secrets and proprietary information that has been at the root of and key to United States economic power.

"There has just been no lessening of activities by the former KGB," Sessions says.

As a result of the decrease in intelligence activities by former East European surrogates of the KGB, the FBI transferred 300 counterintelligence agents to handle inner city violent crime in January 1992. More transfers are expected, although according to Sessions, if the intelligence threat heightens, resources will be shifted back to the counterespionage division.

New Economic Espionage

New threats are emerging from foreign intelligence services. And one of the key issues being examined by the FBI is the growing problem of economic espionage. "I see that problem as being one aspect of those circumstances that may directly affect the security of this country," Sessions asserts. Asked if the problem of foreign government spying on corporate secrets is growing, Sessions replies: "There is strong indications that it does in fact exist. Yes, we are seeing more of it."

He declines to elaborate on the specific sources of the new economic espionage, but adds that the threat "comes from across the spectrum" and includes foreign government intelligence services and foreign companies. "It is not solely from what we would call those countries that formerly fall in the hostile category," Sessions says.

Other officials say the new economic espionage threat is multi-pronged and originates from a variety of countries, including France, Japan, Israel, India, Pakistan, South Korea and Taiwan. European nations that remain close U.S. military allies also are showing signs of renewed interest in economic collection. They include the British, German, Dutch and Belgian governments.

The remaining traditional adversaries, especially the Chinese, Vietnamese and Cuban intelligence services, also pose a continuing threat to U.S. national security, acknowledge several security experts.

CIA Director Robert Gates is acutely aware of the problem. At least two clear-cut examples of foreign government espionage against U.S. corporations have been detected in recent months. Those operations included planting "moles" within corporate structures and breaking into hotel rooms and rifling the briefcases of businessmen who travel abroad.

Tactics, Techniques and Targets

Tactics employed in the new espionage are the same as those used in the traditional game of spy vs. spy. The methods include traditional human intelligence (HUMINT) techniques: planting agents within American corporations who pass trade secrets to foreign intelligence services, who in turn pass them to foreign competitors. There have also been cases where agents did not steal information but served as "influence agents" — corporate executives who can affect high-level decision-making in ways favorable to foreign governments or competitors.

Other methods include the widespread use of electronic listening devices — bugging hotel rooms, residences and even commercial airline seats. There have also been cases where foreign governments have rifled the trash of American corporate executives in a search for trade secrets. Front companies have also been set up for economic espionage purposes, as a means of providing greater access to facilities and personnel with valuable proprietary information.

"With the collapse of the KGB, Japan has taken first place as the world's top exporter of disinformation"

A 1991 survey by the American Society for Industrial Security found that 37% of 165 major U.S. corporations that took part in the review experienced thefts or attempted thefts of corporate secrets, either from competitors or foreign governments. The survey revealed that the data foreign spies covet most include product development information, manufacturing technology and sales and marketing data.

Key technologies under attack include medical and pharmaceutical, semiconductor design, computer software development, chemical processes, aerospace, electronic banking, optics, packaging and telecommunications.

The survey indicated that economic espionage activities by foreign entities jumped dramatically in recent years. Reported thefts or attempted thefts of commercial secrets by foreign firms or governments against U.S. companies grew from only 14% between 1981 and 1986, to 69% between 1987 and 1990.

Another major target of foreign spying is electronic communications, including facsimile, computer transmissions and telecommunications.

Although its use so far is not widespread, foreign government dissemination of disinformation in the marketplace is an area being watched by economic counterintelligence agencies.

"We've seen what can happen if someone discredits an American product overseas," says senior FBI official Oliver B. "Buck" Revell. "If you get intelligence services involved it can have a devastating impact." Since operatives of the former KGB were "past masters" at the use of political disinformation, Russia's use of economic propaganda is one area to watch.

Trade organizations linked to some elements of the Japanese government have been blamed for spreading malicious disinformation about American products whose manufacturers are trying to break into the closed Japanese market. In one case, a film was produced by groups linked to Japan's rice cooperative which alleged that U.S. food products were poisoned and even caused birth defects. The anti-U.S. disinformation has been traced by U.S. officials to some officials of the Japanese Agricultural Ministry.

"With the collapse of the KGB, Japan has taken first place as the world's top exporter of disinformation," asserts John P. Stern, Tokyo vice president of the American Electronics Associations.

In addition to food products, American electronics components and aircraft parts and services have come under attack in the Japanese marketplace. In one case, a Japanese research firm with ties to the government circulated a report among business leaders alleging that certain U.S.-made microchips were defective, when in fact the products were superior to Japanese competitors' chips.

To better cope with the problem, the FBI has revamped its entire counterintelligence strategy. Once limited to investigating spy activities by "hostile" intelligence services, primarily those of the Soviet Union, its friends and allies, the FBI recently adopted a new counterintelligence strategy it believes will help meet the challenges of the 1990s and beyond, including economic espionage.

The new National Security Threat List concept, as the strategy is called, was unveiled in October 1991, by Harry B. "Skip" Brandon, a veteran FBI counterspy. The list outlines eight counterintelligence "issues" which give the FBI greater flexibility in investigating and thwarting spying by any foreign governments, not just the traditional adversaries, but so-called friendly governments as well.

High on the list are the protection of core technologies from foreign spies and U.S. industrial, proprietary or economic information. Any foreign intelligence service that runs operations to acquire corporate trade secrets is now fair game for FBI counterspies.

Brandon — perhaps more than most federal intelligence officials — sees the coming years as a time of increasing uncertainty and one that will challenge U.S. national security in many ways.

"The 90s have already begun an amazing period of transitions and we in the FBI and the Intelligence Community think this is going to continue," Brandon explains. "There will be continued uncertainty, continued changes, a greater range of emerging threats and challenges than we've ever seen before. We think it's going to be a period in which we will see significant changes in the political, military and economic alignment around the world."

Among the key features will be increased political transformation and intense international economic competition, he adds. Priority targets for many foreign intelligence services will be a variety of information, including corporate proprietary data, government classified secrets, foreign policy, military intelligence, and political information and technological plans and programs.

The loss of American corporate secrets to foreign government intelligence services "is in the beginning stages, it is happening, it is escalating," notes Senator Boren. "It is not at a tremendously high level but it's high enough that warning bells ought to be going off about the nature of the problem."

An equally serious problem and one that is more prevalent than economic spying in the United States, is the use of foreign intelligence services to spy on American firms that bid for contracts overseas and that lose out when that information is provided to government-owned businesses competing with U.S. firms for contracts, says the Senate Intelligence Committee chairman.

An additional problem is the outright purchase of American high-technology firms by foreign corporations, a tactic used effectively by the Japanese, he says.

"We could really wake up and find ourselves sitting on the sidelines of the world stage if our economic decline continues, and unfortunately, unfair tactics by others, in terms of espionage intelligence collection, could really badly tilt our ability to compete," warns Boren.

Congressional Hearings on Economic Espionage

Some 20 nations are engaged in economic espionage activities against U.S. corporations, including both friends and foes who have targeted technology, proprietary data and other trade secrets.

"Some governments in Asia, Europe, the Middle East and to a lesser degree Latin America, as well as some former communist countries — nearly 20 governments in all — are involved in intelligence collection activities that are detrimental to our economic interests at some level," CIA Director Robert Gates told the House Judiciary subcommittee on economic and commercial law recently.

Top government security officials, corporate executives and security specialists appeared before the congressional committee on April 29, 1992 to discuss what they said was the growing threat of economic espionage directed against U.S. corporations.

The House subcommittee has been investigating the problem for nearly a year under the direction of Chairman Jack Brooks, (D.-Texas).

"Clearly the risks to sensitive business information are dramatically increasing as foreign governments shift their enormous espionage resources away from military and political targets to world commerce," Brooks said.

"Intelligence agencies from the former Soviet bloc nations and our allies in Europe and the Far East are actively targeting U.S. corporations," he said. "The information they seek is not simply technological data but also financial and commercial information which will give overseas competitors a leg up in the world marketplace."

FBI Director William Sessions said economic espionage by foreign intelligence services against U.S. corporations is not yet a large-scale undertaking. But it is something that will increase in the coming years as a result of intensified international economic competition.

Sessions said the main threat of economic espionage concerns the theft of "core" technologies and proprietary and trade secrets by foreign spies.

Based on intelligence analysis of what foreign governments are seeking, Sessions listed the following critical technologies that are deemed vital to U.S. security and which are targets of foreign collection:

- Manufacturing processes and technologies
- Information and communications technologies
- Aeronautic and surface transportation systems technologies

- Energy and environmental-related technologies
- Semiconductor materials and microelectric circuits
- Software engineering
- High-performance computing
- Simulation modeling
- Sensitive radar
- Superconductivity

It was the first time the FBI has discussed the specific technologies in public.

Sessions also said the FBI is supporting a proposal by the National Security Agency to place curbs on U.S. sales of advanced data encryption systems because they could hamper the ability of U.S. intelligence to fight drug trafficking and terrorism.

Among the nations most active in using intelligence services or government agencies for economic spying are the former Soviet Union, Israel, France and Japan

---

Many U.S. high-technology companies are opposing the proposed curbs on the grounds that they need the best encryption equipment in order to thwart foreign spying.

The NSA wants to restrict sales of the most advanced coding equipment, which is currently available from foreign suppliers, in order to maintain its capability to monitor international communications.

Milton J. Socolar, special assistant to the comptroller general of Congress' General Accounting Office, provided the most detailed testimony identifying the nations involved in industrial espionage. "While it is not possible for me to quantify the scope of economic espionage conducted by foreign intelligence agencies, there is evidence of a real and growing problem," Socolar testified.

Among the nations most active in using intelligence services or government agencies for economic spying are the former Soviet Union, Israel, France and Japan.

Socolar confirmed reports that Israeli agents stole trade secrets from Recon/ Optical, that French agents penetrated IBM and Corning in France and that Japanese government agents have engaged in economic spying.

"The government-to-industry relationship makes it difficult to determine if the Japanese government is involved when Japanese companies successfully acquire U.S. corporate secrets in an unauthorized manner," Socolar said, noting the 1982 case of Hitachi employees who pleaded guilty to conspiring to steal IBM design documents and components.

Socolar said the foreign counterintelligence programs of the CIA and FBI are not well-coordinated and thus do not adequately protect U.S. industry against economic espionage. "Economic espionage must be looked at very carefully," he said. "There should be a thorough review of which agencies should be involved in this area together with what their responsibilities should be."

Gerard Burke, a former NSA official who took part in a GAO investigation of economic espionage, said the recent espionage arrests in Europe were an indication that the new Russian spy agency is continuing the aggressive industrial spying of the KGB.

The governments of China, Japan, France, Israel, Sweden, Switzerland and Britain are among the most proficient at economic spying, Burke said.

Surprisingly, British intelligence may be "the most successful and professional of all" in economic spying, although "the British almost never get caught," Burke said.

Monitoring the Economic Intelligence Threat

CIA Director Gates provided valuable testimony on the nature of the threat and the patterns of activity that have been detected.

"Our fundamental assessment is that while the end of the Cold War did not bring an end to the foreign intelligence threat, it did change the nature of the threat," Gates said.

Many nations are continuing to target U.S. technology, he noted, and are also shifting to include activities beyond technology collection to include a range of economic and business data.

Among the new targets of foreign spies are government policy deliberations on trade, investments and loans and positions on bilateral economic negotiations. Several governments also are spying on private bids for contracts, information that affects prices of commodities, financial data, and banking information affecting stock market trends and interest rates, Gates said.

"In addition to collecting economic information, some foreign intelligence services have tried to exert clandestine influence on U.S. business and government decisions that affect their economic interests — by attempting to recruit agents of influence in U.S. government, banking and business circles," the CIA director said.

One country that was not named, has also been pushing so-called "active measures" — a combination of overt and covert action — to influence publics, governments or businesses, Gates said, without elaboration.

Also, Gates mentioned "heavy-handed" lobbying efforts by several other governments on behalf of state-owned firms that were attempting to exert political and economic influence.

The proliferation of intelligence technologies in recent years has also changed the nature of the threat. Over 50 Third World governments are using the intelligence training they received from former Soviet bloc states to "act unilaterally" in their intelligence-gathering, including in the economic sphere.

The number of professionally-trained intelligence mercenaries who are willing to ply their trade for a price is also growing as a result of cutbacks in the massive spy agencies of the former Soviet bloc.

Gates said traditional adversaries are continuing to conduct economic spying, as well as many industrial nations.

"Some countries with whom we have had good relations may adopt a two-track approach of cooperating with us at the level of diplomacy while engaging in adversarial intelligence collection," Gates said.

The CIA has found several distinct patterns of intelligence activity related to economic spying:

❑ Classic espionage, typical of communist-run countries.

❑ Elicitation of information, rather than recruitment.

❑ "Bag operations" by intelligence services into hotel rooms of executives for trade secrets that are passed to national firms.

❑ Use of government agencies other than intelligence services as part of a systematic information program, largely through open sources, and then passing the information to business leaders.

❑ Use of front companies, military attachés or special intelligence units outside normal intelligence channels to clandestinely obtain sensitive weapons technology.

❑ "Intelligence entrepreneurs" who hire out to foreign governments or private organizations, an emerging pattern.

Gates said monitoring the foreign economic intelligence threat is expected to become a higher priority for the CIA in the coming years.

Identifying purely American interests in this area could be a problem, he noted. "We will need to surmount any conscious or subconscious tendency to apply a double standard — which could lead us to downplay hostile activities if conducted by certain countries," Gates said.

How Industry Views the Economic Spy Problem

James Riesbeck, executive vice president for Corning, Inc., testified about how the glass and fiber optics manufacturer views the economic espionage problem.

"For the first time since the 1930s, the United States is not threatened by a foreign military power," Riesbeck said. "As a result, our stature in the world will increasingly be determined by what is done in corporate board rooms and on factory floors, rather than by the Joint Chiefs of Staff.

Noting that glass technology dates to ancient Egypt, Riesbeck said Corning's success at maintaining a competitive edge has been based on developing new and higher value added specialty products and processes that are closely guarded corporate secrets.

In an apparent reference to French economic espionage, Riesbeck said "Corning has been the target of state-sponsored industrial espionage efforts aimed at our fiber optic technology." It was the first admission by the company that its fiber optics know-how has been so targeted.

Corning's R & D efforts have included a number of products with national importance, including glass light bulbs, television glass, ceramic cores for automobile pollution controls, fiber optic communications, silicone photochromic lenses, and specialty ceramics for space exploration.

"We will survive and remain competitive by continuing to stay on the cutting edge of technological development," Riesbeck said. "We must make sure that our technology is not knowingly or unknowingly stolen by our international competitors."

Industrial espionage by foreign governments is a problem that is difficult for individual companies to counter. "The resources of a corporation — even a large one such as Corning — are no match for industrial espionage activities that are sanctioned and supported by foreign governments," Riesbeck said. " . . . We expect the problem to get worse over time . . ."

The use of "public switched" communications networks for data and voice transmissions has made trade secrets more vulnerable to interception, he said. Riesbeck said he favored the greater use of encryption devices for industry.

Marshall C. Phelps, Jr., IBM vice president for commercial and industry relations, told the subcommittee that unfair or illegal practices by foreign competitors could jeopardize the competitive edge of the U.S. computer industry, which employs 600,000 workers who produce more than $165 billion worth of hardware, software and services annually.

"Among the most blatant actions are outright theft of corporate proprietary assets," Phelps said. "Such theft has occurred from many quarters: competitors, governments seeking to bolster national industrial champions, even employees. Unfortunately, IBM has been the victim of such acts."

As a result, economic espionage has resulted in "losses to IBM in the billions."

Some examples of IBM being victimized include theft by domestic and foreign companies of IBM's personal computer software known as BIOS; theft by foreign companies of IBM's critical mainframe computer secrets; foreign government agents obtaining proprietary information for indigenous companies; and the counterfeiting of hardware and piracy of software.

Chapter 2:

Foreign Governments' Role in Economic Spying

"It would not be normal that we do spy on the States in political matters or in military matters, but in the economic competition, in the technological competition, we are competitors; we are not allied."

— Pierre Marion former chief of France's foreign intelligence service in a televised interview on NBC News program Exposé.

The increase in aggressive economic spying by foreign intelligence services against U.S. corporations has been highlighted by a series of landmark cases over the past several years. These cases have generated intensified interest on the part of both government and industry security experts. According to these experts, these cases are likely to become the predominant form of espionage in the 1990s and beyond.

An examination of the publicly available information about these cases provides valuable insight into the nature of the problem and is a starting point for developing effective counterintelligence awareness and security countermeasures programs.

One of the problems in discussing economic espionage by foreign-intelligence services is the extreme sensitivity of the issues involved. For government, many of the most serious recent cases of economic spying have involved key allied governments, especially those in France, Japan and Israel. For that reason the U.S. government has been reluctant to share with the private sector important details about these cases.

From the corporate perspective, companies that have been victimized by foreign government spying, notably IBM, Texas Instruments and Recon/Optical, derive no financial benefit from discussing their past security failures. On the contrary, negative publicity generated by corporate theft can hamper business. For that reason, American business has resisted public discussion of these cases.

They are explored here for the sole purpose of educating the corporate information executive to the threats and dangers of government backed industrial espionage of the present and future. These examples have been provided by government intelligence and law enforcement officials, as well as corporate security operatives charged with protecting trade secrets.

Since many of the more notorious past cases of Soviet and East bloc industrial espionage have received wide publicity, the focus here will be on the nontraditional intelligence threat — spying by so-called friendly intelligence services. A number of these services are known to assist or conduct economic operations against the United States. They include Britain, the Netherlands, Germany, Belgium, South Korea, Taiwan, Pakistan, and India. But U.S. officials say three nations — all allies — are the most active in conducting aggressive economic spying: France, Israel and Japan. Ultimately as these cases show, intelligence services, like nations, do not have friends; they have only interests.

France's *Direction Generale de la Securite Exterieure*

U.S. officials say France's foreign intelligence service — the *Direction Generale de la Securite Exterieure* (DGSE) — is among the most aggressive of the spy agencies currently engaged in large-scale intelligence operations against U.S. high-technology companies.

The French service has demonstrated it is willing to use all the traditional tools of the espionage trade, from electronic eavesdropping, to penetration agents, to trash surveillance, in its quest to obtain information that will support French industry. Security experts agree that the DGSE represents one of the most serious threats to American corporate secrets.

Far and above many of the recent industrial espionage cases is the story of how the DGSE penetrated IBM France, Texas Instruments and Corning Glass in a daring and risky intelligence operation.

The case began sometime in 1987 or 1988. The scene: the ministerial office of a senior French government official. The topic of discussion among a group of senior officials, including a representative of the DGSE, is how to make France's struggling, government-owned computer firm, Compagnie des Machines Bull, more competitive with international computer makers.

Several years earlier the French spy service had scored one of the West's most successful intelligence coups of the Cold War. A senior KGB officer assigned to the Kremlin's Military-Industrial Commission defected and began working for the French. The KGB man, code-named "Farewell," provided large quantities of information on how the KGB and GRU engaged in a massive covert program to collect Western high-technology from foreign corporations.

The French decided to emulate the KGB methods disclosed by Farewell in their own daring and risky intelligence operation against the U.S. computer giants IBM and Texas Instruments. Using classic intelligence tools of the trade, the DGSE successfully recruited several French nationals employed at the two firms. In one case, the recruited agent was reportedly the number two official in one of the companies. The French affiliate of Corning Glass, which manufactures high-technology fiber optics communications connectors and couplers was also penetrated as part of the DGSE scheme.

Although details of the how the employees were recruited remain unclear, in other cases the DGSE was able to exploit calls to service in the name of French patriotism as a means of recruiting penetration agents. In any case, until late 1989 when the operation was exposed through the joint efforts of the FBI and CIA, French intelligence obtained valuable information about all research programs and commercial strategies of the American computer companies and passed the information along to Bull.

The French news magazine *L'Express,* which first reported the penetration operation in May 1990, said the French agents inside the corporations were interrogated by the FBI during visits to the United States in 1989. Their activities were exposed, the moles were fired, and the entire affair was kept out of the public eye until *L'Express* broke the story. W. Douglas Gow, then chief of FBI intelligence, confirmed the story in a television report six months later. "There was activity on their part," Gow said of the French computer caper.

U.S. officials said the DGSE program to spy on foreign economic secrets was not new. The DGSE's Service 7 has been engaged in economic spying since the 1960s using a broad array of techniques that include insinuating agents into American companies and carrying out large-scale interception of electronic communications. Service 7 also has penetrated a large segment of the French hotel service industry and uses its agents to break into the hotel rooms of visiting executives and copy or steal valuable trade secrets.

Hostile spying by the French intelligence service dates to 1962, when Paris hatched a plot to set up a special scientific and technical intelligence network to covertly obtain U.S. nuclear secrets. Fortunately, the French chief of station in Washington, Philippe Thyraud de Vosjoli, who was to direct the operation, reportedly became a double agent for the CIA and exposed the plan.

Richard Mainey, director of security at IBM, declines to comment on the IBM France penetration but acknowledges that the case had occurred and says "the rules of the game" prohibited him from discussing it in detail.

However, Mainey is willing to outline IBM's corporate security philosophy: "Unlike the Mounties, we don't always get our man," he says "But when we don't, it's generally because of self-imposed limitations on what we do. We do not emphasize finding the culprit as much as identifying the problem and then preventing the problem from recurring."

Stan Victor, a spokesman for Texas Instruments said his company regards the French penetration as a matter between the U.S. and French governments, and the FBI and French intelligence. "We don't want to get into embarrassing the French government," he says.

Also, U.S. officials have said that a recent television interview given by a former French intelligence official about DGSE economic spying was the most startling and revealing admission about the French operations to date.

Tape-recorded conversations are turned over to French intelligence who then monitor the tapes for business secrets

---

Pierre Marion, who briefly ran French intelligence beginning in 1981, disclosed on the NBC News program *Exposé* in September 1991, that he was the one who directed French intelligence to step up spying against U.S. businesses. "It would not be normal that we do spy on the States in political matters or in military matters," Marion says. "But in the economic competition, in the technological competition, we are competitors; we are not allied."

According to Marion, 20 DGSE agents were assigned to a special economic intelligence unit within the French service charged with collecting economic secrets. The targets, says Marion, were documents and intercepted communications. *Exposé* identified the DGSE mole within Texas Instruments as Jean-Pierre Dolait, an executive who was fired by TI in 1989.

Corporate security experts speculate that IBM lost valuable research data that cost the company millions of dollars.

Marion boasts of DGSE exploits in other countries. For example, the French company that makes Mirage jet fighters won a billion dollar contract from the Indian government after French agents secured bidding data from the competition, in this case an American aircraft manufacturer and the Soviet government. "We managed to have a source of intelligence inside the Indian administration," Marion disclosed.

Since the IBM/Texas Instruments case, a number of more recent DGSE intelligence activities have been uncovered. FBI sources claim there are currently several ongoing cases involving French economic espionage.

U.S. intelligence officials confirm that French intelligence has planted hidden microphones near all first-class and business-class seats on Air France flights from the United States to Paris. The airline routinely monitors all conversations of foreign business travelers, and with the help of agents among the airline crew is able to identify targets for eavesdropping. Tape-recorded conversations are turned over to French intelligence who then monitor the tapes for business secrets.

Paris hotel rooms of visiting businessmen also are important targets for the DGSE. In October 1991, for example, two executives of National Cash Register returned to their rooms in the Nikko Hotel to find the doors pried off the hinges. The only items missing were two NCR high-tech notepad computers that contained valuable corporate data.

The most recent case occurred last year in Washington. French intelligence brought over a number of engineers from France and through the French embassy launched a high-technology collection scheme. The DGSE obtained a list of U.S. chemical manufacturers involved in producing the coatings used in radar-evading stealth aircraft. Working from the list, the French engineers, posing as officials of the French nuclear agency, made telephone calls to scientists who worked on the secret technology. They appealed directly to the American scientists to turn over the formulas and processes for the stealth technology simply because France and the United States are allies.

One scientist immediately contacted the FBI, who intervened to break up the French effort and warned the U.S. chemical companies that were targets of the French operation. Officials say the French were careful in selecting their technology collection targets. Instead of seeking the most advanced stealth-coating secrets, the French sought out first-generation technology with the idea that it would not be as well-protected as the more advanced chemical coatings.

France's consul in Houston recently came under FBI scrutiny when he picked up two trash bags in the posh River Oaks section of the city. The garbage was believed to be the waste of a computer executive that may have contained corporate secrets. The consul, Bernard Guillet, denied he was an economic spy searching for computer secrets and says he was only picking up grass clippings to fill in a hole in his front yard. But FBI officials said the trash surveillance was not an isolated incident. French agents have tried to search other executive household garbage in the area.

Israeli Civilian, Military and Scientific Intelligence Services

Although the most recent case of reported Israeli industrial espionage dates to 1986, U.S. officials say Israel is among the most aggressive of the economic spying organizations operating against American companies. Israel has several services that collect economic intelligence, including the Central Institute for Intelligence and Special Duties, known as *Mossad,* and the Israeli Defense Forces Intelligence Branch, known as *Aman.* A special science and technology intelligence collection unit within the Israeli Defense Ministry surfaced in 1985 when civilian naval intelligence analyst Jonathan Jay Pollard was arrested and later pleaded guilty to passing secrets to Israel. Pollard was handled by the Office of Scientific Liaison, or *Lakam.* The unit was a key economic intelligence-gathering service.

A high-profile case of Israeli government-backed industrial espionage surfaced in early 1991. Federal investigators exploring Pentagon procurement practices unearthed details of a sealed arbitration agreement between the Israeli government and Recon/Optical Inc., a Barrington, Ill. manufacturer of high-technology optical goods and Top Secret reconnaissance cameras. The case is illustrative of the type of economic spy operations carried out by Israel intelligence. It is also not an isolated incident.

The case began in the spring of 1986 when a dispute over the costs of a joint Recon-Israeli contract led to a rupture in the deal. Three Israeli Air Force officers working at the Recon plant on a Top Secret airborne spy camera for Israel were caught stealing corporate data hidden in 14 boxes of material being removed by the Israelis that was searched by an alert security guard. Inside the boxes, the guard found a Hebrew-language document which indicated that the Israelis planned to steal Recon's highly-valuable spy camera technology.

The case was taken to a federal court in New York but was moved behind the closed doors of a private arbitration board to prevent undue publicity and to protect Recon's trade secrets from being disclosed in court proceedings. The arbitration board's February 1991 sealed decision was disclosed in a report by *The Wall Street Journal*.

U.S. officials familiar with the arbitration records say they indicated that Israeli intelligence agents, presumably Israeli Air Force intelligence, had used "elaborate subterfuges" to pilfer the Recon optics technology. The Israeli government viewed the technology as "very important to its national security interests," according to officials familiar with the records. The arbitrators described the operation as a sordid affair and ordered the Israeli government to pay Recon $3 million in damages.

Security experts say Israel is among the most aggressive of the economic spies and is motivated by national security concerns as well as a drive for financial gain. Israel depends on its lucrative international weapons sales to fund arms research and development. Israel is also a key supplier of high-technology to China and South Africa.

"Those of us who worked in the espionage area regarded Israel as being the second most active foreign intelligence service in the United States," John Davitt, a former chief of the Justice Department's Internal Security Section told *The Wall Street Journal*.

Israel also is suspected of illicitly acquiring the U.S. technology needed to produce anti-personnel bombs known as cluster bombs during the 1970s. The technology was obtained by intelligence agents and passed to the Rafael Armament Development Authority, which now produces an Israeli version of the U.S. cluster bomb, which carries small bomblets that spread out over a wide area.

The Recon case is one of the clearest examples of how industrial espionage has cost U.S. firms money

---

The Recon case developed out of a $45 million project to build an aerial reconnaissance system for Israel that was funded by U.S. military aid. The project called for manufacturing two high-technology spy cameras, a ground-relay station and a communication network for the package. According to the arbitration records, the Recon security official found that the Israelis had removed confidential technical drawings from the Barrington plant. More important, the Israelis had passed proprietary data to an Israeli defense contractor so Israel could build its own camera systems. The competitor was identified by investigators as the El Op Electro-Optics Industries.

El Op is believed by U.S. officials to have adapted the pilfered Recon technology in its first operational reconnaissance satellite, the Ofek-3. The satellite was launched in early 1992 atop a Jericho II ballistic missile and is expected to provide high-resolution imagery intelligence for the Israeli Air Force the next three years.

Two earlier satellites were prototypes without cameras that stayed aloft only a few months.

Intelligence experts say the Recon case is one of the clearest examples of how industrial espionage has cost U.S. firms money. Every 90-minute orbit of the Ofek-3 around the earth on its reconnaissance mission is a reminder that a U.S. optics firm lost millions of dollars to an Israeli competitor that built the cameras on the satellite without having to pay an American optics firm for its proprietary imagery technology.

The arbitration board reviewed the evidence in the Recon case and said that the Israeli Air Force officers worked closely with El Op in stealing Recon's technology. In fact, El Op asked the Air Force to plant a mole within Recon who could better absorb the high-technology optics information. The Israeli military and industrial officials also discussed cover stories that could be used to protect the security of the operation.

The arbitrators ordered the damages for what they termed the misappropriation of the Recon proprietary data. The key element of the theft was information about Recon's advanced semiconductor microchips that are vital to recording and transmitting camera images. The theft was described by the board as perfidious, unlawful, and surreptitious. Recon came in for criticism from the board for its inadequate information security procedures.

According to the arbitrators, the operation was not sanctioned by senior Israeli officials, but the Israeli government attempted to cover it up and withhold information that could have revealed more about the scope of the operation. The Israeli Air Force officers, were punished, although not for the data theft — they were chastised for letting the operation become public. One of the officers, Motti Harkabi, described as a "direct perpetrator" of the technology theft, soon moved on to another U.S. optics firm, Loral Fairchild Systems in New York, which continued the contract that Recon had dropped.

The Recon case was not an isolated incident. Another major high-technology optics firm and spy camera manufacturer was victimized by Israeli intelligence agents, several years before the Recon case. In that instance, the Israeli Air Force personnel working on a contract with the American camera maker inadvertently exceeded a 50-pound weight limit on a box destined for Israel. A security guard opened the box and uncovered proprietary trade information had been removed illegally by the Israelis. "They just helped themselves to it," says one industry official.

The Customs Service opened an investigation into possible Israeli violations of U.S. export control laws in 1986 but was unable to find out from the Administration if the Recon technology was embargoed and required an export license. U.S. export control policy at the time was dominated by the Pentagon's Stephen Bryen, who is known to be a vigorous supporter of Israel.

Aside from the U.S. optics technology, Israel also managed to obtain procurement documents that helped the Israeli defense industry build its own version of a secret tactical intelligence system known as Joint Services Image Processor, or JSIP. The system facilitates the rapid transmission of imagery data to a ground station which has the ability to integrate the data with other intelligence data. The equipment and software allows optical, radar and infra-red images to be put together. Access to the data would compromise an important intelligence method.

Testimony in the Recon case indicates that Israeli military officials were able to obtain procurement documents on JSIP that resulted in Israel producing a near-exact replica of the system.

Japan's Intelligence Activities: All Business

Most national intelligence services are tasked with the primary mission of national defense. But Japan's spy agencies have a unique aim: Make Japan economically prosperous. Using an array of corporate think tanks, government agencies and semi-private research centers, Tokyo operates more of an intelligence network, rather than the traditional "services" normally associated with foreign spying.

As part of a move to reshape its intelligence operations, Japan's Foreign Ministry and Self-Defense Agency began working in late 1991 and early 1992 to train hundreds of new intelligence analysts and invest large amounts of money in developing greater human and technical intelligence-gathering capabilities. The plans have been discussed publicly but only in vague terms. Japan's national space agency is expected to launch the country's first photo-reconnaissance satellite sometime in the next year, allowing Japan to join the elite fraternity of nations with a high-resolution satellite photographic intelligence capability.

The Foreign Ministry announced that during 1992, an International Information Bureau will be established that will hire up to 200 intelligence analysts to provide information on regional areas of expertise. The Japan Self-Defense Agency is forming an intelligence service at the agency headquarters in Tokyo that will be modelled after the U.S. Defense Intelligence Agency. The unit will focus on gathering tactical intelligence for the defense forces. Japan already cooperates closely with the U.S. National Security Agency in operating several electronic listening posts in the region.

Despite the formation of more formal intelligence organizations, intelligence experts say Japan's network of information-gatherers is uniquely focused on collecting economic intelligence. No other intelligence service, with the exception of the former East German HVA, which specialized in industrial espionage, and the former Soviet KGB, compare with Japanese economic intelligence collection.

The operation is extremely cost effective. The bulk of information collected by the Japanese pays for itself in terms of improving Japanese industry's products and competitiveness. "Eighty to 90 percent of what they do is concentrated on making them more prosperous," says Richard Deacon, British author of the book *Kempei Tai: The Japanese Secret Service Then and Now.* Japan's spy network was set up after World War II using what Deacon describes as "total intelligence," primarily the collection, analysis and distribution of vast quantities of economic information.

A speciality today of Japanese intelligence networks is to identify foreign high-technology companies that will produce valuable products in the future. Japanese industry then sets out to buy the firms outright or seeks control by buying out the firms suppliers.

At the top of the spy network is Tokyo's Ministry for International Trade and Industry, or MITI, which employs more than 15,000 people, compared with only some 5,000 who are employed by the Foreign Ministry. "It's MITI which forges the partnership between government and industry," says Deacon. That relationship is crucial to understanding how the Japanese intelligence-gathering system works. Within MITI, there is the *Keidanren,* or Federation of Economic Organizations, which is a key economic intelligence agency. It sets requirements for information collections, formulates policy recommendations for the government and still serves as a collector of information as well. "It's a very widespread system," says Deacon. "It's not like an intelligence service with one boss. It's spread out to various institutes, organizations and universities."

Among the hundred or so private research organizations that provide global intelligence to the Japanese government-industrial complex are the Nomura Research and the Mitsubishi Research Institutes. These institutes, with offices in major world capitals, employ hundreds of researchers who scour publications and other media for useful information. The data is then fed into databanks, analyzed and distributed.

Other agents buy goods and products from corporate competitors to be sent to research laboratories where they are taken apart and studied and their best features copied or improved. Meetings between Japanese economic intelligence collectors and Western businessmen also are useful for gathering important economic information. Reports are often written on casual meetings and conversations and sent to Tokyo to add to relevant databases.

Herbert E. Meyer, former vice chairman of the CIA's National Intelligence Council, says economic intelligence is integral to all aspects of Japanese business and industry. Japanese trading companies, in fact serve as giant intelligence gathering organizations. These companies, located around the world have developed reputations as world-class spy services that provide vast quantities of valuable information to Japanese industry.

"Much of the activity is legitimate," says Meyer, chairman of Real World Intelligence Inc., in Friday Harbor, Washington, a designer of computer hardware and software intended for use in gathering business intelligence. "But there are times when they do illegitimate activities." Japanese intelligence agents ran secret operations against high-tech firms in California's Silicon Valley in the early 1980s. No recent *sub -rosa* activity has surfaced in public.

Senator David Boren, of the Senate Select Committee on Intelligence, sees another threat from Japanese industry. The Japanese intelligence network targets small U.S. technology firms that are on the cutting edge of advanced technology.

Congress in 1988 empowered the multi-agency Committee on Foreign Investment in the United States to investigate international transactions involving U.S. high-tech firms that might jeopardize national security. Since then, the committee has sent nine cases to the president. President George Bush acted on only one, ordering a Chinese aerospace firm to relinquish ownership of a Seattle machine tools manufacturer.

In November 1991, the federal government began investigating efforts by a Japanese conglomerate to purchase a financially troubled computer firm in Florida that does secret design work, including radar-evading stealth work, for the Defense Department.

"Other governments are seeing where there are gaps and where they can get a real advantage from a technology and simply buying it," Sen. Boren says. "We really don't have a mechanism for protecting technologies that are deemed to be very sensitive for national security reasons from being purchased outright on the open market by a takeover or by a foreign company, maybe even in collusion with their government," a pattern used by the Japanese.

Former CIA Director Richard Helms says the Japanese have shown no hesitancy in engaging in corporate espionage. In one recent case, a major U.S. manufacturer hired a team of corporate security investigators to find out why it had lost three successive and potentially very profitable offshore oil drilling contracts to the same Japanese company. The investigation revealed that the company's computer data, which contained vital bid and proposal data was being siphoned off and sold to the Japanese competitor by a corporate executive.

The data was explicit enough to permit the Japanese firm to construct its bids in such a way that the U.S. firm could not possibly match it. "There was technically not a breach of security systems," Helms says. "No codes were broken, no cipher solved, no high-technology spying was used. It was a plain simple act of bribery, a betrayal for money. Industrial treason if you will."

Other Threats to Trade Secrets: Electronic Spies

Helms uses the example to show a key vulnerability to corporate security and perhaps the most time-honored trick of the trade: co-opting employees with access to trade secrets. "Were I an industrial spy given the task of penetrating a highly secure computer communications system and extracting its secrets, I would not attack the system itself," he says. "Instead I would seek to suborn someone with access to the information I need to permit me to enter the system as a legitimate user. That someone might be an executive secretary, a records clerk or even a trash collector." Once legitimate access is gained, valuable trade secrets can be extracted with little fear that the true owners of the information will ever become aware of the theft. "This scenario is not at all far-fetched."

By some estimates, as much as 50% of overseas telecommunications traffic going outside the United States is transmitted by unprotected facsimile communications. These fax communications have become a major target of international intelligence services and foreign corporations. All that is required for intercepting the fax is a another fax machine that can be plugged into a telephone line in close proximity to the sending or receiving fax machine.

Encryption devices are available to protect corporate fax and telephone communications, but many corporations do not see the need. Noel Matchett, a former National Security Agency specialist, identifies another growing problem. Many companies have begun using electronic data interchange, which is used to transmit corporate bidding, invoice and pricing data electronically overseas. "It helps speed payments, but I think it's just an unbelievably risky procedure," Matchett says, adding that type of data is a major target of corporate spies.

To save costs, some multinational firms are cutting security corners by abandoning private international telecommunications networks and hiring foreign communications networks for its communications. Gillette, for example, recently signed up with British Telecom's Global Network Service which gives the British firm access to its corporate communications to some 20 countries. The British are known to be covert collectors of economic information about U.S. firms.

Chapter 3:

Should the CIA Spy for Corporate America?

"We must have intelligence to thwart anyone who tries to steal our technology or otherwise refuses to play by fair economic rules."

— *President George W. Bush*

The growth of spying by foreign intelligence services that target U.S. trade secrets has prompted a debate over whether the CIA and other agencies should engage in the collection of foreign corporate data and supply it to U.S. companies.

The debate over how to "level the playing field" of international competitiveness in response to economic espionage has two sides. There are those who say that because the French, Japanese, Russians and others are targeting U.S. firms, U.S. intelligence must respond in kind.

But many experts say the legal, ethical and practical problems of sharing secretly acquired foreign trade information are insurmountable and clash with traditional capitalist principles.

One school of thought says the CIA, National Security Agency and other military and civilian intelligence agencies should engage in economic intelligence collection and pass foreign trade secrets to U.S. corporations.

Former CIA Director Stansfield Turner, who ran the agency during the administration of President Jimmy Carter, has no reservations about tasking U.S. intelligence to go after foreign trade data. The former CIA chief has called for a closer, symbiotic relationship between the worlds of intelligence and international business.

According to Turner the preeminent threat to U.S. national security comes from the economic sphere, not military might or hostile political ideologies. With a faltering economy, the U.S. government must redefine its national security interest in ways that give economic strength more importance, he says.

"That means we will need better economic intelligence," Turner wrote in the Fall 1991 edition of the journal *Foreign Affairs*. "The United States does not want to be surprised by such worldwide developments as technological breakthroughs, new mercantilist strategies, sudden shortages of raw materials, or unfair or illegal economic practices that disadvantage the country."

Turner argues that bolstering U.S. economic strength means making U.S. businesses more competitive in the global marketplace. To do that requires sharing intelligence obtained secretly on such subjects as general business trends to inside information on the sealed bids foreign competitors of U.S. corporations offer on international contracts.

To those who say such practices distort the free-enterprise system, Turner responds: "The United States, however, would have no compunction about stealing military secrets to help it manufacture better weapons."

"If economic strength should now be recognized as a vital component of national security, parallel with military power, why should America be concerned about stealing and employing economic secrets?" Turner asks.

A second school of thought, currently discussing the issue of what role the CIA and other agencies should play in economic intelligence gathering, argues against sharing intelligence that will give U.S. corporations a competitive advantage.

The Best Offense is a Defense?

Instead of equalizing foreign economic spying by pushing for a new economic intelligence collection role, the argument put forth by these intelligence experts, including the top levels of the Bush Administration, is this: The best way to level the playing field is to prevent foreign spies from stealing U.S. trade secrets.

Michelle Van Cleave, Assistant Director for National Security Affairs in the White House Science office, sees ethical and legal considerations as the biggest obstacle to a U.S. intelligence role in economic spying.

"For the most part information that is of use to the U.S. private sector is not intelligence per se. It is information that is openly available and information that the private sector by and large is in a much better position to obtain than the U.S. government," Van Cleave says.

The specific question of providing intelligence to the private sector raises a variety of ethical and legal concerns, according to Van Cleave.

"The biggest one from my perspective is truly the ethical concern: I do not believe that the people of the United States would support the United States government being in the business of industrial espionage," says Van Cleave. "Certainly this administration would not support such an undertaking under any circumstances."

It's not just that U.S. spies are averse to risking their lives in conducting operations for, say, General Motors. Ultimately, traditional industrial espionage is an illegal activity carried out by one element of the private sector against another, according to Van Cleave. The practice is contrary to the laws, ethics and values of this country, she says.

A legitimate concern for U.S. business is the problem of foreign intelligence services using their resources to covertly and illicitly acquire corporate secrets from

American firms. According to Van Cleave, there is a modest amount of this kind of activity going on, and to the extent that American business cannot deal with the most sophisticated aspects of this threat — particularly the use of high-technology eavesdropping or communications intercept devices — then government can play an important role in advising the private sector about its vulnerabilities and the economic espionage threat environment.

What really counts in terms of economic competitiveness is not secret information, but using material available from open sources with sound business judgment that will make a difference in the world marketplace. Ninety-nine percent of what is needed to be competitive as a nation can be learned on the playing fields of free markets and through free exchanges, information that has very little to do with the world of intelligence.

The Role of the National Security Agency

A central, albeit secret, player in this debate is the U.S. National Security Agency, the vast, multi-billion dollar signals intelligence collection agency.

NSA is one of the few U.S. intelligence agencies that currently has the statutory authority to collect economic intelligence. According to the law establishing NSA, among the types of intelligence information the agency is authorized to collect through its various eavesdropping programs, "commercial" information is explicitly spelled out.

The agency conducts large-scale electronic eavesdropping around the world on telephone communications, radio signals and other electronic emanations. It routinely intercepts information from foreign governments, including American allies in Western Europe and Japan, that would be of immense value if shared with American industry. NSA also penetrates and monitors international banking and financial institutions for intelligence that would be relevant to U.S. national security.

But sharing that information outside government is something NSA appears unwilling to do.

After press reports in 1990 stated that the NSA was considering a shift to economic intelligence-gathering for American business in the post-Cold War world, Vice Admiral William O. Studeman, the NSA Director said in a rare public speech that doing so was out of the question.

The NSA had no plans to spy on foreign business and economic markets and give the intelligence to U.S. business, Studeman said. Although the issue is being studied, any final decision will not be made by NSA and is not expected for several years. "There are a substantial number of legalities and ethics problems with the concept of trying to provide economic information to businesses," Studeman said. The problem is compounded by the fact that many business are owned by international corporations or rely on substantial amounts of foreign investment. "How do you choose who you are going to give the information to?"

The primary economic role played by NSA is to collect economic intelligence relevant to defense needs and to protect economic information belonging to U.S. businesses such as banks and the federal treasury. "We will definitely help out in defense, but you can leave out the allegations about the NSA spying on friends," he says.

Economic Espionage Consensus and Controversy

The House and Senate intelligence oversight committees are investigating what role, if any, U.S. intelligence should play in economic espionage. The House Judiciary and Congress' General Accounting Office also are engaged in major examinations of the issue.

Richard A. Best, Jr., a national defense analyst with the Congressional Research Service, analyzed the issue in a December, 1990 report. The report, *The U.S.*

Intelligence Community: A Role in Supporting Economic Competitiveness? is one of the few recent studies to examine the issue.

According to Best, the question of providing sensitive intelligence data to businessmen is highly controversial. But there is a general consensus that there needs to be a greater emphasis on economic intelligence.

The question of economic intelligence gathering by U.S. intelligence agencies is a complex one that will confront both the Executive and Legislative branches of government in the coming years, Best says. "The answer to this question should in large measure be dependent upon the needs of the American business community, and that community's awareness and articulation of those needs," Best concludes. "It will also depend on the ability and willingness of the Intelligence Community and those who manage and oversee its work to accommodate such needs while continuing to meet other long-standing requirements from within the federal government."

Regarding the question of providing communications intelligence to U.S. business, Best believes this is one of the most sensitive aspects of the entire question. "Making communications intelligence available to the private sector could entail complicated legal issues and compromise important collection techniques."

Under a 1950s federal statute, it is technically illegal to disclose information obtained through communications intelligence. Also, the use of information collected through clandestine means in the business community would necessarily entail the likely risk that the source of the information would be exposed, thereby limiting future collection.

According to Best, U.S. intelligence has the capability to provide competitive intelligence on foreign companies directly to American firms. But doing so would require an official government industrial policy. Under such a policy, the Intelligence Community could be tasked to provide specific support to designated industries. Such intelligence could be passed to selected businesses, or to trade associations.

But protecting the sources of the information once it reached the business community and choosing who should receive it would raise difficult issues and lead to charges of favoritism, and inevitably legal action. The question of partial or complete foreign ownership and the multinational character of many American firms would also make it difficult to share intelligence directly.

The Public's Need to Know

A second alternative would be to make economic intelligence available to the public, an option that would require enhancing the current outlets and government databases on general economic trends or specific industry analysis. Such an approach would preclude the transfer of the most sensitive economic information, such as foreign competitors bidding data or other sensitive financial data. Under this option, the Commerce Department would play a much greater role in coordinating its unclassified economic information program with the intelligence community.

Currently, a number of federal agencies disseminate scientific and technological information. They include:

Commerce Department: National Technical Information Service, reports by the Bureau of Export Administration, International Trade Administration, and Japanese Technical Literature Program.

Defense Department: Defense Technical Information Center (reports available to some contractors and some libraries); Information Analysis Centers; Defense Intelligence Agency (a database); U.S. Army European Research Office; U.S. Army laboratories; U.S. Army Foreign Science and

Technology Center; Office of Naval Research; Naval Intelligence Support Center; U.S. Air Force Foreign Technology Division.

Department of Energy: Monitors foreign science and technology developments.

Department of State: Some reports by science attachés posted in embassies.

Other government economic monitors include the National Aeronautics and Space Administration, Central Intelligence Agency and National Science Foundation.

CIA Counters Plans to Cooperate

CIA Director Robert Gates has been outspoken in his opposition to any economic intelligence relationship with U.S. business. "I would be very much against that," Gates said recently. The proper role for U.S. intelligence, according to Gates, is threefold:

First, intelligence agencies can identify countries that use their intelligence services to spy on American corporations and collude with foreign business competing against American firms. Second, intelligence agencies can monitor high-technology developments around the world and assess their impact on U.S. security. And third, U.S. intelligence can play a role in thwarting the activities of foreign intelligence services that operate illegally against American companies.

"It think it's not an appropriate activity for us. That kind of activity could quickly embroil us in an enormous legal hassle in terms of advantaging one company over another, or one industry over another," Gates says.

Richard Stolz, the CIA's Director of Operations from 1988 to 1990, put it more bluntly: "As far as Toyota's 1996 model plan, if anybody wants to know, it's up to General Motors to find out, not the U.S. government or the CIA."

Senate Intelligence Committee Chairman David Boren suggested there is a unique role for U.S. covert action in the economic sphere. If aggressive foreign intelligence services continue to operate clandestinely against U.S. firms and fail to heed U.S. warnings, then U.S. intelligence could be used to retaliate. Failing to take any action would be tantamount to unilateral disarmament, he says.

One possible option for dealing with persistent foreign economic spies is the selective use of covert action. "If some country just kept doing it to us and wouldn't do anything else, then maybe we should just steal one of the secrets of one of their companies and publish it in *Scientific American* or something like that where the whole world would have the benefit of what had been only theirs, just to show them, don't mess with us, don't do this anymore," Boren says. Such limited retaliatory action would prevent them from taking action and serve as a deterrent to others. Boren made it clear he is not advocating the practice, only raising it as something to be considered in the debate.

Chapter 4:

Competitive Intelligence Programs Target U.S. Business Secrets

"Most executives don't know what they should keep secret and what they should let go public; an American chief executive will go down to Wall Street to push the stock up and tell the company's whole plan."

— Herb Meyer, Chairman, Real World Intelligence

The phone is ringing on the desk of a manager at a telephone installation company, one of the largest vendors of central office switches in the U.S. He picks up the receiver and a researcher invites him to participate in a survey of man-hour requirements for bringing the central office switches of large manufacturers on-line.

The manager agrees — like the lonely Maytag man, too few call — and soon he is rambling on about a new personal computer-based, computer-aided design system that one manufacturer is using for installation of its switch's documentation, regaling the researcher with the wonders of this feature and how it makes trouble-shooting a nearly push-button operation. Meanwhile, the researcher types madly on the computer in front of him, receiver jammed tightly under chin, plying the manager for details.

Once the survey is complete, the researcher prints out his notes and walks them across the office to his boss, the chief of research who will collate the material from his staff of interviewers who are working the phones. The next afternoon this research group informs its client about these features of that competitors' product that it didn't know about, a nugget that would probably be sent right down to the company's executives for consideration.

The New Agents of Information

Call it espionage or competitor intelligence research, the fact is that these calls are being made every day by companies — or the research groups they contract — and there's no law against what they do. These new agents of information, the men and woman behind the phones and computer terminals are the vanguard of a still-emerging corporate enterprise — and an emerging industry all its own — called competitive intelligence (CI). With that one phone call, the switch manufacturer retrieved as much information about its rival's product as it would have if it had used a more cinematic approach appropriate to the stereotype of corporate spy.

Any collection of information about competitors, just a decade ago, was dismissed with a sneer as spying, something that exists on the same moral plane as peeking into your neighbor's mailbox. Corporate America, seeing the advantages it gave its overseas competitors and hearing the admonitions from academia, have embraced the concept at an accelerating pace. Books by Michael E. Porter of Harvard Business School and other authors have given CI its own vocabulary, that of commerce and information science, and legitimized it as a legal and mostly ethical enterprise.

If corporate intelligence really were espionage it might be a lot simpler to combat. However, since the lion's share of the work is building pictures from disparate bits of information by inference and extrapolation, it's nearly impossible to totally stop. Every company, no matter how careful, leaves information behind in the same way that a battleship leaves a wake or a submarine a sound signature.

Companies as diverse as McDonnell Douglas, Helene Curtis, AT&T, Xerox, Kodak, Digital Equipment Corp., Coors Brewing, NutraSweet and Corning have invested directly in developing their CI-functional departments. No identifiable industry sector has not adopted CI. Smaller companies have also embraced CI. Real World Intelligence of Friday Harbor, Washington, has seen such an interest in corporate intelligence from small firms that it has developed its own $90 software package called RADAR. The software organizes a developing intelligence plan by creating an intelligence profile — defining what the company wants to know — constructing a collection and data management method and intelligence delivery protocols. Companies of every size have apparently realized the power of knowing what is going on around them and in their competitors' businesses.

How fast is CI growing? Probably faster than one might suspect. In 1987, the first meeting of the Society for Competitor Intelligence Professionals (SCIP) was convened. Fifty people attended. In 1992, membership is up around 1,600. SCIP, which has over half of the Fortune 500 represented in its membership, was organized to assist members by enhancing their firms' competitiveness through a more thorough — yet ethical — understanding of competitor behavior and CI strategies.

As an intra-corporate discipline, CI is still in its infancy and many companies are launching CI units every day. The largest fraction of SCIP's membership, 38%, reported in a recent survey that their company's CI unit was less than one year old. Most of SCIP's members are CI officers at large corporations.

Smaller companies, although they may not have the resources to staff full-time CI units, have identified CI's role and assigned the CI function to existing personnel. Leonard Fuld, president of Fuld & Co., Inc., an independent corporate intelligence firm established in 1979 in Cambridge, Mass., says smaller companies are often better practitioners of CI than the giants. Fuld says they know what they want, know what to do once they get it, and the essence of the information collected is not lost from filtering it through layers of bureaucracy.

The acceptance of CI roughly follows the same path of development as "quality control" in the American automobile industry in the 1970s. The concept was considered vital by everyone, yet it wasn't broadly applied until Japanese auto makers demonstrated how it could give a manufacturer a powerful competitive edge. Who can forget the response of a Chrysler vice president interviewed by David Halberstam in his book *The Reckoning* when the author asked him who is in charge of quality control? He shrugged and answered, "everybody," then stammered and quickly corrected himself admitting at last, "really, nobody."

The Japanese emphasis with quality control was scoffed at by the American auto industry of the 1970s as "fit and finish" — a gimmick roughly as important to the function of the car as a good wax job. Quality control, however, became the mantra of American auto makers of the 1980s.

When Lee Iaccoca took control of Chrysler, he made a commitment to quality control expressed as a drive-train guarantee that covered the car for five years or 50,000 miles, an extraordinary warranty at the time that is now almost standard in the industry.

Ironically, when Iacocca was at Ford in the 1970s, he had all but abandoned quality control, relegating it to the dealers who would handle defects and manufacturing flaws. A lot of Ford automobiles made it off the lot in those days — but too many just barely — contributing to a prejudice among some U.S. car buyers that Fords are troublesome cars. Ford, recognizing obvious flaws in its manufacturing process, also launched its "Quality Is Job 1" advertising and quality control campaign in the 1980s.

Japanese corporations, with a keen sense of the power of getting new products to market fast, have built a great deal of their corporate wealth and success on importing foreign technology and ideas. Japan's Mitsubishi, one of the world's biggest conglomerates, has two floors in New York City's Pan Am building devoted to the collection and analysis of business and industrial information. Agents sift and collate primarily public domain materials for transmission back to Japan for consideration by the home office.

Corporate Intelligence is Winning Converts

Corporate America's initial resistance to adopting CI into the decision-making infrastructure was a combination of pride and ignorance, stumbling blocks to many powerful ideas. First, many executives believed their years in industry conferred upon them a prescience that didn't require any information-gathering assistance. Some may have been right about that, but not many. Second, corporate executives have long had the impression that CI is nothing more than a euphemism for spying. While there are ethical dilemmas that CI officers find themselves unable to resolve, the rudiments of CI, knowing the market and knowing your competitors, require little sleuthing, but rather, the workaday vigilance and intellectual curiosity of a district attorney or a good reporter covering city hall.

Yet, CI as a concept is apparently winning converts faster than quality control if SCIP's numbers are a reliable indicator. Quality control is the stuff of statistics. In the example of cars, building better automobiles shows less on the showroom and more in the customer's checkbook. Success is measured over a period of time and monitoring the many snafus that may crop up is hardly engaging. CI, on the other hand, can be exciting, offering at times information that can be immediately useful.

Kodak prevented Fuji from cornering the disposable camera market in the United States with some masterful intelligence work. Fuji's CI section had turned up Kodak's patent for their 35-millimeter disposable, and quickly brought its own into market in Japan. Kodak put together enough information to understand that Fuji was going to bring a version of the disposable snap shooter into the U.S. and got its own version to market just a day before Fuji's reached the shelves, saving the company from loosing substantial profits on a camera of its own invention.

That kind of story — a dramatic, intriguing narrative with profit-saving results — gets around and draws attention in executive circles in a way that more mundane issues such as the rates of repair do not. Executives are closed-mouthed about the investments they make to CI, but SCIP reports that the top 60 corporate users of intelligence committed more than $30 million to this practice. It may be expensive but the biggest players have decided it is well worth the expense.

Profile of an In-House CI Operation

Staffs of CI units that corporations assemble come from many venues but the most prominent is the corporation's existing staff. In intelligence, as in politics, context is everything. Developments in any given industry may be a parade of unrelated events to even the most astute scholar of economics. To an old hand, they have meaning and import all their own.

The closer an observer is to his company, the better able he is to make a call on what an event will mean to his employer. The biggest part of vision is knowing what you're looking for. Still, many intelligence professionals, now that the field is established, come from academia, moving into CI positions after earning advanced degrees in library science, economics, business or in sciences related to the industry where they will be employed.

The chief of McDonnell Douglas' intelligence unit is a longtime aerospace professional with more than 30-years experience in the industry. Senior Principal Specialist Bob Margulies spent most of that time in systems analysis, strategic planning and marketing at McDonnell Douglas, giving him an intimate grasp of his company's place in the market, its weaknesses, strengths and, most importantly, its institutional goals.

McDonnell Douglas, a maker of military aircraft and civilian airliners and transport planes, established its CI unit in 1986 by direct order of Chairman of the Board, Sandy McDonnell. That support from the very top of the company, Margulies believes, was vital in the success of his unit. The initial commitment put nine analysts under Margulies. During a reorganization of the company, though, the unit was reduced to just two. With any less of a commitment from the top, it would have been much easier for the company to write that staff out of the budget.

Margulies and his staff of one are the eyes and ears of McDonnell Douglas, plowing through the datastream every day, alert to market possibilities and new challenges like navigators in a storm.

There is no such thing as a routine for Margulies' CI unit but there are priorities in its mission that have to be fulfilled every day. The overall focus is to keep abreast of the competition's activities and monitor the external environment and identify either opportunities or threats.

When new information is in hand, the CI unit analyzes it and determines what the implications means to the company. This kind of monitoring is simple to perform, requiring an intelligent scanning of the latest newspapers, news services and the aerospace trade journals that are the eyes of industry at large. Margulies says, "If we feel it is significant enough we send a spot analysis [to the appropriate executive]."

One specialty of Margulies' CI unit is keeping tabs on the highest-level executives of its competitors, probing their philosophies, their strengths and weaknesses. That way it allows McDonnell Douglas to predict the course of its competitors should some senior exec die and be replaced by another. Knowing the replacement executive's ideas on aircraft design, manufacturing, and market direction would be valuable information while tracking his power to direct the energies of his company.

Management assigns a lot of the projects that come across Margulies' desk. Managers have their own sources and theories on the market, too, but at McDonnell Douglas, these managers have the opportunity to have their ideas and market scoops investigated and tempered by CI professionals whose research can endorse them and lend them a heartier credibility.

Margulies says his unit is usually inundated with requests for research and organizing all that work is sometimes problematic. The solution is to prioritize the requests by weighing them against the issues facing the company. The requests that address aspects of the highest priority issues get tended to first.

The McDonnell Douglas CI unit draws from a multitude of sources. Printed materials such as books, journals and on-line databases provide rapid retrieval of breaking news and background information. Margulies says the unit also finds materials and new sources in seminars and symposiums.

Although the unit depends heavily on industry sources like suppliers and customers, the most often tapped human resource is the pool of employees at the company. The expertise in any aerospace field is available inside McDonnell Douglas. Those same experts have their own contacts with contemporaries in other companies and, of course, the all-important perspective on events in their own special areas of the industry.

In this way, the CI unit is an organizing force for the information that is already there to be collected, acting as a brain for a nervous system that has to be organized before it can yield intelligence that can be used for profit by decision-makers.

Competitive Intelligence Rules of Engagement

No business CI unit is exactly like another but there are competitive intelligence functions that are common to most. These shared attributes include:

- **Benchmarking** — In a general sense, benchmarking is the process of comparing one company to another. More precisely, benchmarking involves focusing on a specific aspect of a competitor's functional operations and identifying ways to achieve best of class in those areas. That means looking at all the aspects of how a competitor markets a given product or service: people and plant and materials delivery, then comparing it to one's own company. A savvy CI unit will identify where the competitor excels — say in shipping and receiving — and then compare its company with a business in a noncompetitive industry. Essentially, the CI unit in this enterprise is costing out some part of the competitor's business.

- **Competitor profiling** — Creating a profile of a competitor enables the CI system user to better assess a competitor's strengths and vulnerabilities. This provides the basic information that makes change meaningful, giving context to the market's fluctuations. This is an ongoing process and, to some in the industry, the very core of the CI function. Primarily, competitors keep updated profiles of their rivals in order to understand their own place in the market. Often, a CI staff is called upon to profile other companies to judge their quality as a possible acquisition.

- **Assessing competitor capacity** — Judging a competitors' ability to move into a market by determining the plant capacity and cost of their operations is an especially useful measurement when gauging how quickly competitors would be able to get their own products to market after one's own company has engaged in product introductions.

- **Environmental monitoring** — This function is as simple — and as challenging — as looking out for openings in the market where there are opportunities for the company to make money. Street vendors perform a rudimentary form of business climate monitoring when they read the weather report, find torrential downpours predicted, and load up on umbrellas for the next day. In the corporate context, an example of savvy environmental monitoring might be more complex. A tire company watching its competitors would be able to keep up; but one that has gotten information about exciting new lines of inexpensive small cars being imported from Eastern Europe would be able to get the new vehicle's tire specifications and introduce replacements, or seasonal variants, and would be better positioned to sell their drivers some new rubber when the time comes.

Some CI critics emphasize environmental monitoring as more vital than competitor monitoring. Those critics condemn CI as too competitor oriented, reducing the observing company's standards to those of its competitors and in the bargain missing out on the opportunities that the market holds.

The methodology of collection and analysis is also very highly evolved. Today, most CI consultants speak of a three-step analysis system. When new information is in hand it is not yet usable. Raw news is simply data, until it is processed into a usable format. Then it becomes information. When it is analyzed and massaged so that it has meaning, that is the point where it becomes intelligence — information that is actionable. What actions are called for?

There are two generic decision applications that are formed by CI: strategic applications and tactical applications. The strategic use of information speaks to an understanding of where the corporation should go from the portfolio standpoint, such as which business areas and what size products the company should engage in developing.

Tactical use of CI is for more immediate market concerns like how to reduce your company's product manufacturing costs relative to your competitor to gain market share. Of course, CI's most prevalent application is in tactical situations since the market is always offering up new challenges that require rapid deployment of new information.

These are generic applications that address a broad range of issues facing a company. The kinds of questions that these kinds of inquiries answer address many vital corporate activities. Think about what you'd like to find out about your competitors or the market environment and know this: your competitors are probably wondering the same thing.

The specific questions most asked by companies seeking intelligence about their competitors, according to the independent competitive intelligence group Washington Researchers, Inc., include:

❑ What is the company's overall strategy? The information to answer that question would allow a competitor to know where its rivals were heading in the market — and to enter the market before the competitor.

❏ What is the financial picture, including detailed breakdowns of costs and sales for specific divisions and products?

❏ What new product or services are in development?

❏ What new markets are targeted?

❏ How are certain areas of the company staffed and structured — especially sales and R&D professionals.

❏ What do they really want? What's the bottom line in their quest for more information?

A poll taken last year by the American Society for Industrial Security (ASIS) on corporate theft — not a valid function of CI, but a telling indicator of the kinds of information that competitors want — shows that the leading genre of information that competitors want is clearly product development.

Respondents reported that product development information was the target in 154 security breach incidents. Manufacturing technology was the second most sought after item with 84 attempts. A poor third was basic research with 27 attempts. The poll results indicate that the closer to market a product moves, the more attractive information around that product becomes to unscrupulous competitors.

A Wealth of Information Just for the Taking

Where do they get the information to answer these questions? Mostly from the target companies themselves.

Financial reports required by law of publicly traded companies, such as annual reports and 10Ks hold a wealth of information. Intelligence analysts have highly developed mathematical formulas that can divine a company's strategy by calculating its distribution of capital resources — drawing on information largely from these public documents. Information from the local government provides other public documents like building plans for new plant construction and modification that have to be filed. All can be incisively informative to a CI officer.

Next, is the promotional and consumer material that companies produce — brochures, advertisements and product advisories. After that, is the softer — yet often more vital stuff — the news in the industry press from the supplier, about a big load of materials going to a new start-up. Finally, there are the stories from the vendors told over coffee at trade shows and in phone calls to a dealer.

Yes, those phone calls are the most productive vehicles of information transfer, any CI practitioner will admit. That method often yields the most timely and useful information. Large corporations, however, are wary of calling their competitors for legal and public relations reasons. They'll often contract with outside corporate intelligence agencies to do some of the telephone interviewing. Time after time, employees will drop what they're doing and give away the farm — not knowing the "ultimate" consumer of the information they are blithely giving away.

The Push to Integrate CI into the Corporation

The functionality of CI is not new but the act of chartering it as its own enterprise is a relatively recent phenomenon. The push toward integrating CI into the decision-making cycle came from the U.S. academic community that has studied how the country has lost market share in key industries to offshore competitors. Finding, inspecting and analyzing information about competitors didn't carry the stigma there that it did on the corporate side.

Smart corporations have been marshalling the observational powers of its staffs for a long time, the way an editorial writer calls in senior reporters for an informed assessment of the issues of the day before he or she forms and writes an opinion.

Yet it wasn't until CI began to gain credibility as an essential industrial function as important as "R&D" and "marketing" that corporations began staffing formal CI units whose duties were to guide the corporation through turbulence and, more importantly, steer them to the opportunities in the marketplace.

Implementation of company-wide intelligence systems requires more reorganizing of existing resources than it does acquiring new resources — probably one of the reasons it's coming into acceptance so rapidly. Increased quality can cost any amount of money one may want to spend. Information retrieval is a comparative bargain.

CI has evolved to a point where developmental strategies for implementing it as part of an overall corporate plan have been standardized. Even analysis regimes have become nearly standardized.

R.I.M.: The Three Stages of Development

Development of corporate CI plans generally follow a three-step stage of development — recognition, implementation and maintenance — according to W.R. Welsh, director of marketing at Pacific Bell:

Stage I, the recognition stage, is when a company discovers that it needs to create a means of moving information around the company that concerns markets in which the company is competing, usually when a company gets burned by a competitor's coup or, very often, when an employee's analysis predicting such a market upset has been ignored by decision makers due to a lack of any systemic vehicle for transmitting such market information.

Welsh estimates that by the end of the recognition stage, corporate officers and other functionaries will acquire new roles, defined by their place in the intelligence infrastructure. Having these roles assigned will cut down on lags between market events and the company's response time.

Some intelligence consultants organizing a CI unit begin by identifying the qualities of information which each corporate officer collects — and the information each needs. From there, they can construct a dataflow system into which authorized employees contribute and whereby each corporate member will be delivered needed information.

Intelligence specialists also perform one essential yet rudimentary organization miracle: Collate existing documentation and computer data into a form that is accessible and expandable. Nothing new is added, just shaped into new tools that make intelligence gathering possible.

Stage II is where the work of intelligence gathering begins to happen as the corporation begins using business intelligence in its day-to-day business. Sharing a "support system" within the company reduces uncertainty throughout the organization, Welsh believes. The result after the second stage of development: Proactive planning becomes possible and departments know where to go to get the information they need.

At Stage III, business intelligence is adding value to the enterprise by eliminating duplicated work, and reducing time to market, according to Welsh. Users of business intelligence are in touch with each other and those who need information have their bucket in the datastream.

The CI plan can be created by assigning new roles to existing staffers or by creating an independent intelligence office — usually the route only large corporations can afford. These roles define the flow of information and create a functional framework for CI activities.

Corning, the glass maker, has transformed the entire company into a massive data-collection lens, adding almost no new staff when integrating its CI plan into the corporate structure. Absolutely everyone, from the salesmen to the highest executives are expected to file reports when they come across usable information.

Corning, a model of today's intelligent corporation, has developed a computer environment just for its intelligence system, based on a network of DEC minicomputers and software for database management and videotext retrieval. At any time, an employee can contribute information to the Corning system and it will find its way to the appropriate party in the company.

When a corporate intelligence plan is in place, it is less a part of a company and more a part of the orchestration of company functions, connecting far-flung parts of an organization that may never have worked together. All of the great intelligence work in the world is wasted unless it is delivered to the corporate officers who can use it.

Gary Roush, manager of information management at Corning, likes to tell a story about one of the company's buyers who had seen crates of glass-making material on a dock addressed to a competitor factory. He mentioned this fact in his trip report and one of their engineers was able to figure out what kind of glass the competitor company was planning to manufacture. This is an example of CI at its simplest — and at its best.

Chapter 5:

Information Gathering Techniques Used by Competitive Intelligence Analysts

"What you're doing when you're assessing a competitor is creating the best possible picture. You can get most of the dots and get a good picture . . . You'll have enough to put it together and see what it all means."

— *Leonard Fuld, President, Fuld & Co., Inc.*

World War II Navy Captain Ellis Zacharias is an unlikely hero in the competitive intelligence (CI) field of the 1990s but today his principles of intelligence gathering are the totems of the enterprise. "There is very little that confidential agents can tell that is not accessible to an alert analyst who knows what he is looking for and knows how to find it in open sources," he wrote in his book *Secret Mission: The Story of An Intelligence Officer*. Zacharias defined the operative role of the corporate intelligence agent: The collector with an interpretive eye who can extrapolate important new insights from readily available information.

Competitive intelligence works for companies the way memory and powers of analysis works for individuals; a few shreds of information regarded by an intelligent observer can yield the facts. It is just this deductive nature of CI that makes it practically impossible to stop, given the vast amounts of information that companies disclose in the course of doing business.

Information transfer is one of the risks of doing business in the age of CI. In most industries, no company can be totally information tight.

However, if today's companies are to develop their own counter-intelligence judo for fending off the intrusions of competitors, they must understand that knowledge of their corporate strategies and vulnerabilities is of paramount interest and can be valuable weapons in the enemies' arsenal.

In some instances there is a darker side to competitive intelligence work — situations where the line between espionage and intelligence gathering is blurred and ethical ambiguities are left unexamined.

The richness and availability of Captain Zacharias' "open sources" to which all corporations contribute one way or another, make CI a process all but impossible to halt — or resist. Hiding from the enemy was easier in Captain Zacharias' era because these days, the trackers on the heels of corporate America have better resources and skills than any World War II intelligence unit ever had.

Black, White and Gray: The Art and Craft of CI

The information gathering techniques that are employed by corporate intelligence agents fall into roughly three categories: the black, the white and the gray, colored according to their propensity to expose their practitioners to ethical lapses and unlawful transgressions.

The black episodes are the ones that make the headlines when they are discovered and agitate industry representatives victimized by them to call for Congressional investigations of corporate espionage. These are by definition illegal operations, involving interception or theft of trade secrets by such means as electronic eavesdropping or buying confidential information from a corrupted corporate source.

The white approach is untroubled ethically though no less informative than other modes of collection; the above-board, dogged research is where a lot of the work of corporate intelligence is performed. The lion's share of information at this level of information collection comes from materials often available in public libraries.

Some of the most important pieces of the puzzles CI units reconstruct come from that gray area of the corporate intelligence enterprise, however, where the ethical boundaries become blurry, where collection modes are technically legal but, if exposed to the light of day, would cause some pangs of an embarrassed, belated conscience to the company engaged in collection. It is here, in the vast, gray dataspace where the CI agents hide behind their telephones, where a heightened sensitivity by employees to the preciousness of the information they work with could save companies from substantial losses. People are the most important asset of any corporation and, at the same time, the greatest potential liability in terms of information security.

The art and craft of working in the gray area of corporate intelligence work has a lot to do with getting people to help put information into focus or disclose those pieces of the puzzle that available resources don't reveal. That means getting people to talk to a stranger about information that is the lifeblood of their companies. A poll completed in 1991 by the American Society for Industrial Security (ASIS) showed that humans are still the most prominent way for secret information to leave a corporation, followed by discarded trash, computer and telecommunications networks respectively.

Most all of the aggressive digging by CI agents can be counteracted in the corporate environment by instituting a single command: Thou shalt not speak to strangers. "Strangers" in this context refers to callers whose identity has yet to be verified. No company would want to allow unauthorized persons to have access to the computers where its information is stored. This same rule should apply to the most dynamic storage agents: the company's employees.

Keeping A Lid on Company Secrets

Every employee has the potential to harm his employer by injudicious disclosure, but there are certain key corporate employees that all CI professionals relish capturing on the phone for an interview. These are the functionaries that companies should warn about giving away the family jewels:

- Marketing personnel. Knowing where the product is going, how it's going to be sold and what new products are in the pipeline are all within the marketing department's purview. Also knowing where the competition's interest lies is within their job description in many corporations. A well-placed phone call to one unguarded marketing department could yield vital information about many competitors.

- Sales personnel. By nature of their jobs, these people are gregarious, talkative and informed, a triple threat to the company that wants to keep its secrets secret. Sales reps are knowledgeable about pricing of products and, more importantly, new products and developing sales campaigns.

- Public relations/investor relations personnel. Their job requires that they be curious and knowledgeable about their companies and receptive to customer or investor requests for information. A lot of the information they impart is publicly available, but the best of them can put that information into context rapidly for a caller. They can make it easy for an investor to make up his mind on staking some shares — and just as easily help a CI agent stake out the company.

- Corporate library personnel. Trained to give out information and having access to most everything anyone would want to know about the company, the librarians are the institutional memory of any company.

- Purchasing agents. The astute CI professional often taps these people to gauge the costs of competitor's supplies, raw materials and services. That kind of information is important in extrapolating costs of production and for developing a cash flow model of the target corporation.

- Plant managers. No one knows how products are put together better than these employees, the real captains of industry. CI agents tap into plant managers to find out costs on production, plant capacity, production equipment and percentage of the plant being used.

- <u>Union representatives and shop stewards.</u> Organized labor uses intelligence techniques as sophisticated as any CI professional in calculating a company's capacity to pay wage increases. They often have the best information on pay scales, staffing levels at different installations, the level of employee training and overall hiring practices. Unions also are knowledgeable on how much work — and which kinds of work — are bided out to sub-contractors, a big part of the equation for high-maintenance industries like telecommunications.

Control of information inside a corporation would be a simple matter if so much of business wasn't bound up in doing business with other companies. Even if a company could get complete control of its employees' tongues, CI agents would still have plenty of outside sources to use to get inside information on competitors. Consider how much information these agents have concerning their associated businesses and their motives for sharing:

❑ **Customers.** Customers are the experts on pricing and volume discount rates; think of the value that kind of information is to your competitors. Remember, any individual who knows your business or any part of it, can be an information asset for any competitor collecting information on your company.

❑ **Suppliers.** Suppliers are always willing to ingratiate themselves to a potential client and customers are always looking for a better deal, or a chance to benchmark their costs of materials and services. A talkative supplier can give competitors all kinds of information on production plans, new equipment introductions and rates of consumption.

❑ **Vendors.** Unless a company sells off its product through its own sales force, there will be vendors out there with almost as much knowledge of manufacturers' products as the manufacturer itself. Vendors often sell competing products in the same category, allowing a CI agent to get intelligent comparisons with a single phone call.

Not all the CI professionals are constantly working the phone. They are stalking about, antennae alert, at trade shows, seminars, conferences — even Congressional hearings — anywhere information about competitors might be disclosed.

More than half a million companies exhibit at trade shows somewhere during the business year. Before the advent of the age of CI, it was considered sleazy and disreputable to hang around the competition's booth. Now, it's more or less expected. Smart companies keep an eye out for probing visitors.

Seminars and conferences are other likely venues where CI agents in one place can make fast contact with many sources. Speeches by executives may often reveal enlightening clues to their companies' strategies if they don't assume that their competitors are listening. They are. The exchange of news and a little swaggering public relations is also a natural part of such events. CI agents also play on the networking atmosphere to find new contacts. When wine flows, secrets slip.

Talkative employees and business contacts that have been engaged for an interview by a CI professional share one common trait: They have no idea who is the ultimate consumer of the information. (There have been cases where executives and managers have given away secrets to their competitors while teaching at colleges and universities local to their base of operations. Rivals would send their CI agents to the class to listen and take notes, entitled to hear the thoughts and experiences of an esteemed professional just like any paying student.)

For a moment's skepticism and curiosity about the identity of people in the audience, the corporate speaker could be rewarded by further questioning the questioner before deciding on an ambiguous response that compels silence. CI professionals are skilled at leaving their company or clients' names unknown or cloaking it with subtly misleading identifiers. For most of the CI industry, that is an ethical dilemma it has learned to live with — and flourish by. Some have called it the industry's sin of omission.

Gary Roush, manager of information management at Corning, Inc., tells a story about a phone call he got one day in 1991 from an "MBA student". The caller said he was researching Corning for his thesis and a professor had given him Roush's name. Roush did a little questioning himself after he got the caller off the line. Sure, he was a student, a night student. By day he worked for the competition as a manufacturing manager, something he forgot to tell Roush.

Even for the most experienced CI professional, there is a stunned disbelief at what people will tell them, an amazement at employees' generosity and unguardedness about information that they work with.

There are many tried and true interview-initiation techniques that have been developed over the years. Each can be defined in how close it comes to disclosing the identity of the ultimate consumer of the information that the CI agent is collecting.

CI agents sometimes will identify themselves, their company and their position accurately and simply start barking questions. Some just identify themselves by their own names and plunge into an interview.

Hiring Free-lance Information Mercenaries

Many large corporations have external CI units and give them names that target companies would not identify with the competitor. They sound like authentic think tanks — and many are — but when it comes to crucial information about the parent company's competitors, they have all the independence of a bank-owned appraisal firm.

When companies don't want to expose their own CI units or external research firms to compromising situations, they will often hire independent research companies whose agents can call and accurately identify themselves with nary a pang of conscience. (Big companies interested in making contact directly with a competitor usually are directed by corporate counsel to hire contractors for two reasons: the potential liabilities under the anti-trust laws on communications between competitors and, of course, the public relations liabilities of getting caught.)

Competitor intelligence groups get a lot of work from the space between the anti-trust law and the chance of getting caught. Still, tacitly deceiving interviewees by failing to inform them of the ultimate consumer of information being collected — such as the scenario in the beginning of Chapter 4 — could be considered unethical.

There are researchers who will completely missidentify themselves and lie about the destination of the information they are collecting. Among the bogus IDs they most often proffer are journalist, market researcher, trade association researcher looking for statistics, a customer or a potential customer, an investor, a stockbroker, a materials supplier salesman and a student doing a research project. Of course, some CI professionals are more creative than others and may have invented even more innocuous sounding identifications.

Why do people talk? Human beings are the only creatures that are known to tell stories. All they need is an audience to motivate them to narrate, opine and inform. Some, no doubt love to talk about things in areas of their expertise that may be taken for granted in the context of a large, compartmentalized corporation; call this one the Maytag syndrome. Corollary to that is the fact that, for employees, being in on industry developments is exciting and the pleasure of speaking about them is increased proportionately to the employee's proximity to the events.

Some talk because the interviewer has appealed to the employee's vanity. The caller finishes his introduction and lets on, that his research department has identified him as an important expert in his field. Who wouldn't give such a wise and discriminating caller a moment?

Remember that people are social creatures who exist through a ballet of cooperative efforts; consider the number of cooperative transactions that it takes simply to get a glass of wine to a dinner table in a restaurant. It's hard for one person to turn away another who is asking for something we have the capacity to give. This is the human dynamic at work when an employee agrees to offer information to a friendly caller who has humbled himself to admit his ignorance and ask for information.

Employees might also operate under the delusion that what they know is everyday, mundane information everyone around the office — and therefore the world — knows. Who knows how many final pieces of the puzzle were dropped into place by an employee who took his company's information for granted?

An unguarded employee might respond positively to a query about his company's international trade, its dollar value and percentage of sales, thinking what does it matter. But a CI officer with a calculator could quickly calculate total sales and domestic sales, offering some figures useful for comparisons — or for even more mathematical extrapolations.

The one "talker" that no amount of education can silence, however, is the disgruntled employee who will talk to get a lead on a job from a competitor. Often, employees will volunteer information to callers from the competition to send out feelers on possible employment there. This kind of behavior generally increases in direct proportion to employee morale.

The rule of survival in the age of CI is know who your employees, managers and executives are talking to — and why.

Combing Through Competitive Information

Call this the white vector of corporate intelligence. For the bulk of the information, the stuff that provides context for corporate profiles and industrial events, the CI officer needs to employ no trickery. Information gleaned from public sources like newspapers and periodicals can all be enlightening, depending on the enterprise level of the publications. With electronic databases like NEXUS and DIALOG, words are forever — and never before have they been so easy to retrieve. Much material is also being packaged and sold on CD-ROM, allowing companies to access vast amounts of relevant data on a computer.

Some other sources that CI analysts comb regularly include:

- <u>Law suits.</u> Depending on the case, most any corporate secret may "have" to be revealed to prove a point.

- <u>Press releases.</u> Unless scrupulously sanitized, they can reveal a wealth of information by themselves or in conjunction with other publicity materials and marketing brochures. Related companies can often spill the beans on each other. A packaging company issuing a press release on say, a new screw top carton, could tip a company's hand on a new juice product release.

- <u>Building inspector reports.</u> Specifications drawn in floor plans could reveal enough about a manufacturing site that competitors could divine what a company is planning to make.

- <u>Securities Exchange Commission filings</u> — specifically the 10K and 10Q — offer a wealth of late-breaking information on publicly held companies. Combined with other information, these reports can be used to discern cash flow models that can point to vulnerabilities in the target company.

- Mortgages and Universal Commercial Code listings. These are filings required to register collateral on loans and can expose the borrowing practices and indebtedness of target companies.

All are readily available through open sources, and chock full of material providing enough pieces of the puzzle to allow the astute observer to draw many accurate conclusions.

For example, Coors Brewing, an active and early CI practitioner, was able to take advantage of a lawsuit that was brought against one of its competitors. Coors' intelligence staff collected some numbers from the discovery proceedings and calculated how many barrels of beer its competitor brewed — accurate to within one percent. No spies involved, nothing cinematic but the agents were able to uncover a vital piece of inside information. All it took was a careful consideration of the available facts and a mathematical model designed to make these disparate figures speak to the larger issues — like how much beer their competitor is making.

Anything that is printed in an open source has the same power to illuminate a larger issue. CI agents plumb many secondary sources for the tail that reveals the cat. Among these are:

❑ **Help Wanted advertisements.** Competitors can divine what a company is planning often by simply learning the kind of personnel that are being courted. A supermarket manager spotting his competitor up the road advertising for a pastry chef wouldn't have to think too hard to conclude his competitor is expanding its baked goods section.

❑ **Requests for bids.** The materials, sub-contractors and services that a new venture requires can easily reveal its intent.

❑ **Company newsletters, speeches, and executive testimony before Congress.** The unguarded disclosure — that is one that doesn't consider that the competition is part of the audience — can be very damaging.

EG&G, the contractor which operates the nuclear materials plant at Rocky Flats, Colorado, published in its own newsletters, safety regulation violations at the plant that led to its closure — referring to them by code number. The Denver office of the Associated Press was able to send a reporter out to the community college nearby where back copies of the newsletters were kept. The code numbers of the safety violations in the newsletters were looked up in the regulation books, revealing the actual violations. The AP wrote more than one dozen explosive, damaging stories based on facts it found in a publicly available newsletter.

The IBM customer list story is a parable many hold out as the event that gave birth to market research and corporate intelligence in America. A disloyal IBM public relations officer one day in the mid-1960s left his office and walked to Grand Central Station with the company's customer list, as the story goes, and copied it on a public coin-operated photocopy machine under the station's big clock. It was a time when the computer industry was ready to grow and new players wanted to enter but the market was owned by IBM. What better way to discover the market than that list?

The turncoat PR man sold it to an unknown party who brought it to a copy store whose employees alerted IBM security when they read "IBM CONFIDEN-TIAL" stamped on the document. IBM security tracked down the parties who'd bought the list back to a college dorm room, confronted three young men, and retrieved the copied list — but not before copies had been handed around. The three men? Principals and associates of the market research groups that sprouted around that era.

Details of this parable vary with the teller but one thing is true: somehow the lists were secreted away from IBM. Some are still in circulation, on the shelves of market analysts, journalists and industry insiders. The real power of the tale is not in the accuracy of its details but in the points that it makes about the nature of the industrial information collection enterprise. There are ethical boundaries that can easily be breached by any employee with devastating results, displaying how fragile corporate security really is and how easily the CI enterprise can integrate with corporate espionage. Indeed, it was the CI community that had to explain why what it does is not espionage.

The Tricks, Tools and Technologies of the Trade

Though the CI community has powerfully made its point that its enterprise can be ethically impeccable and of vital service to industry, the techniques and technologies for espionage have never been growing faster.

Though the James Bond image of the techno-agent has polluted the perception of what espionage is all about, it is people with sticky fingers doing most of the spying. An ASIS study revealed that 40% of the theft incidents involved outsiders, 12% involved insider acting alone and a whopping 48% involved outsiders and insiders acting in concert.

The methods involved little technological sophistication. They included: removal of information from offices, theft of customer lists, bribery of employees, theft of trash and unauthorized reproduction of documents.

The conclusion is obvious: The first place any employer should look for corporate spies and espionage activity is right on their own payroll.

Security experts advise that all employees be screened carefully, and previous employment references prodded for all information about the candidates, and employees' careers. Any "holes" in the resume should be immediate cause for suspicion and for vigorous investigation. That period of missing time on the resume could be the interval during which that employee candidate was working for a competitor — and maybe still is. New hires should be required to read and sign a binding confidentiality agreement.

As well, security experts advise, employees leaving a company should be completely debriefed, reminded of their confidentiality agreement and called to account for all records and computer files in their possession during their term of employment.

Now that the gauntlet of CI has been thrown, no company can consider itself safe. The tools of knowledge have proved too useful, too important to go back to fighting blind. It is a protracted battle, a siege of wits, that can temper a corporation or destroy it. Countering CI, still, will never be a war of absolutes in terms of winning and loosing but rather another of the many risk management chores to which all companies must attend.

Chapter 6:

Are Laws Adequate to Protect Corporate Secrets?

"Prevention of industrial espionage is better than attempts to avenge or remedy it. Litigation, not merely in the U.S.A. but almost everywhere in the Western world, is a costly quagmire into which none but the brave, the wealthy or merely foolhardy dare venture."

— Peter Heims, author of "Countering Industrial Espionage"

A s threats to the secrets of American companies increase abroad and at home, managers frequently look for protection from the law. The statutes that cover business secrets are filled, however, with gaps. Some of the threats are so new—whether due to new technologies or new business practices—that the law has not yet caught up. Even when it has, the risks of litigation are large and the costs often very high. Prevention remains the only certain way to safeguard information.

Abroad, American firms increasingly form alliances with foreign-owned companies. Often, these links require sharing business secrets. How can a company protect these secrets? It needs protection not only from outright theft but from mishandling that can result in unintentional but nevertheless devastating disclosures.

Foreign laws concerning business secrets vary greatly. Often they do not provide adequate protection. While some countries, for example, do not allow an employee to exploit information about customers which is gained before termination, others do allow it. Some countries do not allow lawsuits to recover damages. Even in some that do, injunctions are not available to defend against further abuse once a case of mishandling is discovered.

U.S. businesses normally require licenses from foreign companies before they expose any sensitive information. These agreements identify types of information that are to be protected, the kinds of confidentiality they require, and sometimes the sorts of penalties for breaches. Differences in law, however, may sometimes make it difficult to enforce these contracts in foreign courts. American companies usually consult local attorneys before signing licenses and factor their possible unenforceability into the calculation of business risk.

Trade secret protection is an important element of several international trade agreements currently being negotiated by U.S. representatives. Such agreements are not a panacea. The language sponsored by Washington does not fill all the gaps but is designed to provide what one official calls "minimal protection."

Significant differences will still remain among signatory nations even after the agreements are ratified. And the dealings of foreign intelligence agencies, unscrupulous police or inefficient courts may thwart enforcement even when the law itself is sound.

For this reason, American companies try to convince U.S. courts they have jurisdiction, even in cases involving foreign companies and foreign countries. U.S. law is more highly developed in the trade-secret area than in most other countries. Still there are gaps in the law even here at home.

Trade Secrets and Other Intellectual Property

In American law, trade secrets are distinguished in the law from other kinds of intellectual property that a company tries to protect, such as patents and copyrights. Although a company has certain legal rights to each, the latter differ in being in the public domain, while a company's trade secrets are not.

And while all of a company's patents are technological in content, only some of its trade secrets are. The rest are what might be called proprietary business information—such things as business strategies, investment plans, bids, studies, and other kinds of nontechnical information.

The range of legislation and legal practices dealing with the protection of a company's information assets is wide, various and sometimes complicated. A smart corporation will draw on the advice of lawyers at all stages of the preparation and execution of an information protection policy.

Some statutes already protect a company's intellectual property, such as its computer data, and make unauthorized access to it or its theft a crime. Other statutes give a company leverage in prosecuting civil claims against those who pilfer its trade secrets, but only when the company has created a serious program to protect them and can demonstrate this to the courts.

It is not prudent for a company to expect the legal system to do all the work of protecting its secrets

---

Judges apply guidelines established through custom and legal precedent in deciding if an item of information is protected as a trade secret. Lawyers can tell a business when the law can and cannot assist against competitors' acquisition of proprietary information.

Moreover, when a company has the law on its side, the best legal advice may be against litigation, since publicity surrounding a court action could threaten company secrets as much as any thief. Lawyers familiar with federal administrative law can assess the risks associated with placing trade secrets in the government's hands. And they can warn overzealous security officials away from practices which protect information in ways that violate the law.

The protection of trade secrets takes place in a world defined by lawyers. A company should know that world. A prudent company acts within the law and uses the law for its benefit. But the law is not everything. It is not prudent for a company to expect the legal system to do all the work of protecting its secrets.

Protection and Gaps in the Criminal Law

The criminal law protects trade secrets in a number of ways. At the federal level, the theft of trade secrets is covered by a variety of general laws rather than one single statute drafted for that purpose. Consider what happened to Merck & Company.

In March 1991, two men were convicted in Newark for peddling stolen drug formulas. They had been targets of an FBI sting. One, a former Merck chemist, tried to sell an undercover FBI agent a 29-page report loaded with Merck trade secrets, plus a frozen sample of the firm's genetically-engineered microbes used in a fermentation process for an animal health product.

The chemist and his confederate also thought they might sell the FBI man a secret technology to produce the anti-cancer drug Interferon, stolen from a second drug firm, Schering-Plough Corporation. The unprecedented FBI operation had involved hidden microphones and cameras, an FBI front company and meetings from Atlanta to New York City.

The Merck case was prosecuted as a violation of mail and wire fraud laws. Such a strategy is applicable to many other trade-secret cases, since conspiracies to steal business secrets usually require some form of fraud—such as when the thief is an employee who clandestinely uses his position of trust with an employer to obtain and use the employer's confidential information for personal gain.

Statutes prohibiting interstate transportation of stolen property also apply. However, federal courts have ruled that only tangible property can properly be said to have been "stolen;" the mere taking of ideas across state lines does not violate these laws. Moreover, recent court decisions suggest that some business information, such as the data in discarded or recycled documents, is beyond the reach of theft statutes because the documents containing the data are no longer owned at all and thus cannot be stolen.

The recently enacted Computer Fraud and Abuse Act of 1986 makes it a crime to enter computers or to manipulate or copy the data inside them without proper authorization. Critics, however, have pointed out holes in this law, too. The language sometimes makes it difficult to prosecute creators of computer viruses, for example. Moreover, it may not be a crime under the act for someone to misuse a computer so long as the individual is authorized to have general access to it.

Legislation at the state level fills in some of these holes. A number of states have enacted legislation specifically aimed at trade-secret theft, and these laws usually define a broader range of theft than exists at the federal level.

Consider the experience of Procter & Gamble. In late 1991, Cincinnati police ordered the search of over 800,000 phone toll records after local Procter & Gamble officials had reported an employee's leaking of unfavorable news about the company to *The Wall Street Journal*. Ohio law prohibits employees from disclosing a company's secrets.

The investigation was unsuccessful. Worse for the company, a flurry of negative publicity followed the disclosure of the police action. It forced the company's chairman to admit in a letter to employees that Procter & Gamble had made an error in requesting the search.

In many states, it is possible to steal ideas and penalties for doing so are comparable to those for stealing tangible property. In some states like Ohio, as the Proctor and Gamble case shows, the law makes business practice information potentially subject to trade-secret protection. Where there are no specific statutes, general fraud and theft laws still apply, just as they do at the federal level. Still, the numerous differences in the criminal law of trade secrets as one travels from state to state reflect gaps that some critics argue should be filled. At present, the best a company can sometimes do is to turn to the civil courts.

Civil Lawsuits and Reasonable Actions

Through civil litigation, a company can sometimes sue successfully to gain an injunction stopping the improper disclosure or use of a trade secret, or where that is too late, to require thieves to pay a reasonable royalty if they continue to exploit the secret. A winning lawsuit may also require the thief to pay monetary damages, covering both direct losses and punitive costs, as well as attorney's fees.

The courts consider a number of factors in determining whether a piece of company business information warrants legal protection as a trade secret. How extensive is the knowledge of it inside and outside the company? How novel is it? How distinct is it from the special talents and general knowledge of the company's employees?

The legal precedents in the trade-secret area differ so much from state to state that in 1979 the National Conference of Commissioners on Uniform State Laws proposed a Uniform Trade Secret Act to standardize the legal practices. This proposal has gained increasing acceptance as the basis of individual state statutes protecting proprietary business information.

The commissioners codified the practice of most of the states by recommending that a piece of information satisfy two key guidelines to qualify as a trade secret: (1) that it derive "independent economic value, present or potential, from not being generally known," and (2) that it be "the subject of efforts that are reasonable under the circumstances to maintain its secrecy."

Companies therefore should be interested in the security around their proprietary information not only to prevent its theft but also to obtain the full benefit of the law in punishing thieves or receiving damages from them.

In his book *Trade Secrets,* lawyer James H. A. Pooley has identified a number of reasonable actions that the courts have come to expect of a company that makes the accusation that trade secrets have been stolen.

- ❑ Does the company control access to its facility?

- ❑ Are there rules about what can be removed from the facility? Are measures taken to enforce those rules?

- ❑ Are there security guards?

- ❑ Are employees identified by badges?

- ❑ Do they have other identification?

- ❑ Are there restrictions on visitors' access to the facility or to parts of it?

- ❑ Are particularly sensitive documents stored under lock and available only under supervision?

- ❑ Are employees required to sign confidentiality agreements?

Written agreements are important beyond the assurance they give the courts of good-faith efforts to protect information. On their own, they represent a further level of legal protection. Unlike the criminal and civil statutes cited so far, ad hoc agreements are not generally governed by the legislation and judicial precedents surrounding trade secrets but rather by their own provisions and by the law of contracts.

Agreements come in a variety of forms. By a technology license agreement, one party grants to another party the right to use some form of technology or technical information. The licensor will specify what is licensed and what is not, and will normally obligate the licensee to protect the technical information and often indemnify against its unauthorized disclosure. Visitor nondisclosure agreements may be required of visitors to a secure facility, pledging them not to disclose proprietary information to which they may be exposed.

Finally, confidentiality agreements by employees and contractors place explicit and detailed restrictions on what can be done with information acquired on the job.

These agreements are of two kinds. Nondisclosure agreements obligate the signer not to disclose specified categories of information obtained in virtue of his or her employment and acknowledged by the signer to be owned by the employer.

Noncompetition agreements obligate the signer not to compete with an employer for a period of time; they protect information by making it hard for an employee or business associate to profit by having it. Noncompetition agreements are unenforceable in some states. In the case of agreements of either kind, theft of trade secrets is handled as a breach of contract.

While some laws require a company to exhibit an active program of protecting trade secrets if the courts are to recognize cases of theft, other laws place constraints on what is permissible in such a program. It is prudent for security officials to devise programs in coordination with company attorneys to guarantee that they remain within the bounds of the law.

Noncompetition agreements, for example, are ordinarily enforceable only when they are reasonable; it is thus unproductive to have employees sign unreasonable agreements, and it may be counterproductive as well, if they are relied on in lieu of other measures.

Eavesdropping equipment, like hidden cameras and microphones, and electronic monitoring devices, such as those used to listen in on telephone conversations, have been the targets of civil litigation even when legally used. It is sometimes smart for a company to have employees sign waivers granting the company the right to use such equipment, but lawyers should carefully scrutinize waivers to determine their enforceability.

Polygraphing of employees by private companies is prohibited by federal law except when a crime is thought to have occurred; lawyers should closely supervise their use. The courts do not recognize a right by an employer to search employees or their possessions; waivers may again be needed, a company's search policy should be well-publicized, and lawyers should be involved in all searches.

Litigation Sometimes Difficult, Risky

But while a company must act within the law in protecting its secrets and should always act to receive the full benefit of the law, no company should rely on the legal system alone for protection. Certain kinds of information are unprotected by law. In general, only trade secrets are protected, and even there, only secrets satisfying customary rules or belonging to categories covered in legislation. Nontechnical business information is often not protected, much less the nonsecret information that a clever competitor can compile from public sources without inside sources.

Even when a kind of information is covered by the law, the process of prosecution and litigation is still unreliable: victims do not always win. And even when they do win, the cost may be high. The financial cost of litigation may be prohibitive.

Moreover, to go to a criminal prosecutor about a theft of secrets is to give up control over the litigation process. The company's lawyers no longer call the shots;

government prosecutors do. This may result in the very loss of information the company's actions were intended to prevent.

Although the attorney-client privilege is generally recognized and company relationships with certain other categories of professionals may be protected in some states, the confidentiality of business relationships is not generally a right, and secrets may spill into the courtroom during testimony.

Part of the defense's strategy in the Merck case was to maintain that the allegedly stolen material was in the public domain; if the defense had prevailed, not only would the government have lost its case but the drug manufacturers could have lost their secret drug formulas.

Even in civil lawsuits, these are real dangers. Although the Uniform Trade Secret Act has a provision to preserve secrets against unnecessary publicity, there is no guarantee that a plaintiff will always be successful in this.

Chapter 7:

Corporate Computers — Information Gateways at Risk

"We are at risk. Increasingly, America depends on computers. They control power delivery, communications, aviation, and financial services. They are used to store vital information, from medical records to business plans to criminal records. Although we trust them, they are vulnerable — to the effects of poor design and insufficient quality control, to accident, and perhaps most alarmingly, to deliberate attack. The modern thief can steal more with a computer than with a gun. Tomorrow's terrorist may be able to do more damage with a keyboard than with a bomb."

— From "Computers at Risk: Safe Computing in the Information Age," a report by the National Research Council.

These days, when law enforcement officials round up the usual suspects following the commission of a computer crime, they are just as apt to get their woman as they are their man, according to a study by the National Center for Computer Crime Data (NCCCD), a Los Angeles research firm.

"Computer crime is an equal opportunity employer," says Buck BloomBecker, director of the NCCCD. The results of the survey indicate that women and minorities are increasingly as likely to commit computer crime as young white males.

The knowledge needed to perpetrate computer crimes is spreading rapidly through the population. "Increased access to computers is also increasing computer crimes, not only in the hacker community but across the board," BloomBecker says. The survey found that 32% of those arrested for computer crimes are women, 43% are members of a minority group and 67% are between 21 and 35 years of age.

Most computer crime — whether it is the unauthorized access to a company's files or the planting of a logic bomb designed to destroy programs and data — is likely to be carried out by current or former employees.

According to some experts, at least 61% of frauds are instigated by employees; compared to a mere nine percent of the crimes that are linked with outsiders. The primary security problem stems from the complacency of senior management, apathy and ignorance that pervade most computer-using organizations, they say.

"The wise computer security professional will worry less about hackers and more about employees," BloomBecker says.

Computer criminals aim to steal money and services when they break into a computer system electronically. The two categories make up 70% of computer crimes.

"The most important characteristic trend in the area of computer abuse is what isn't happening," BloomBecker says. While the proportion of cases referred for prosecution tripled in 1989, the last year figures are available, only six percent of "serious computer security incidents" is actually being reported, he says.

The Costs Of Computer Crime

Computer crimes committed by current or former employees, hackers, who modify data for fun, "phreaks" who steal telephone service and others are costing U.S. industry billions of dollars annually.

Surveys that attempt to estimate the magnitude of computer crime by number of incidents or by costs vary widely. The National Center for Computer Crime Data estimates computer crime losses at around $500,000 per year. Ernst & Young, meanwhile, puts the annual cost of computer crime at between $3 billion and $5 billion.

"I think both figures show that this is not a trivial problem," says BloomBecker. "The real problem is not reflected in dollar losses" but when users are hindered from using computers, "which is a difficult thing to estimate."

Whatever the costs, it will probably take even greater losses before industry and the government devise a coherent strategy to combat it, in the view of law enforcement officials, legal experts and industry researchers.

Here are two of the key reasons that computer crime remains less than a priority:

First, "computer crime" resists definition. For one person, it is any crime directed at or taking place within a computer; for another, it is any crime in which a computer is a tool of the crime.

Second, businesses report only a small percentage — about six percent, by one estimate — of criminal acts aimed at their computer systems, for fear that publicity will be bad for business or attract copycat crooks.

Without any kind of national consensus on what computer crime is and how much it costs, there is no appreciation for the magnitude of the problem and thus no incentive on the part of business and government to do anything about it, several experts say.

Compounding the problem is the propensity of industry and law enforcement to blame each other for failing to take stronger measures to combat computer crime. Information systems security managers complain that when they report crimes, the bulk of offenses go unpunished. Law enforcers often lack necessary skills and are too slow to investigate and prosecute computer crimes, they say.

"Where do corporations go for justice?" asks an information systems security manager. "Unless the crime is over $500,000 — better still, over $1 million — they won't even give them the time of day."

Computer crimes are difficult, time-consuming and costly to investigate, and in the face of other crimes, have a low priority, law enforcers admit. "Computer crime just doesn't stack up against murder," says Ken Citarella, assistant district attorney for Westchester County in White Plains, N.Y. He also heads the district attorney's computer crime prosecution team.

"If someone comes in with any kind of crime, it has to be evaluated to see whether to expend resources, for its impact on the community and the need for it to be prosecuted," he says.

The problem lies in the failure of businesses to report crimes in the first place, Citarella adds. It is not likely that local government will allocate tax dollars to combat computer crime if law enforcers cannot point to a mounting case load.

The Difficulties of Investigating and Prosecuting Computer Crime

When a competitor stole a tape containing a copy of Phase Linear Systems' top mainframe software product from a Phase customer, executives at the Phoenix-based firm naturally went to the police. However, the lack of a serious attempt by local authorities to investigate and prosecute the case has left the company executives wondering why they even bothered to report the crime in the first place.

The case remains unresolved, even though the culprits are known and have admitted taking the tape, says Phase general manager Tom Darcey. "The police advised us that the theft of a $10,000 piece of software was a low priority," Darcey says. "To them it was an inexpensive reel of magnetic tape, but to us it could have been a disaster because it doesn't take much to figure out that the competitor would analyze the program."

Law enforcement officials at local and federal levels admit they have their hands full with a wide range of serious crimes and say that computer-related crime is not a high priority. However, they also argue that they are more willing and able to investigate these crimes than in recent years.

It is just that the job is a lot bigger than anyone had ever suspected. Computer-related crimes are time-consuming to investigate and hard to prosecute, says Gail Thackeray, a former Arizona assistant district attorney. Computer crimes that include telecommunications fraud extend across state and federal jurisdictional boundaries, thus making collaboration on an investigation difficult. Telecommunications carriers are often unwilling to cooperate for fear of violating privacy laws that could allow the criminal to sue.

Virtually every case is larger than it first appears and often involves several criminals in several states, Thackeray says. One case involving a hacker group that made repeated attempts to take over a hospital computer system took nearly 18 months to investigate, which is typical for most crimes of this sort. Members of the group eventually were convicted about a year after the investigation was completed.

During the past decade, there have been only 250 prosecutions of computer-related crimes, according to U.S. officials.

More stringent and technically precise laws are sorely needed, especially on the federal level, according to many legal experts.

The Computer Fraud and Abuse Act of 1986, a key federal crime-busting statute, is ambiguous and does not adequately cover the broad range of computer-related crime, says Joseph Tompkins, a partner in the Washington, D.C., law office of Sidley & Austin and chairman of the American Bar Association's Criminal Justice Section Task Force on Computer Crime.

"There is ambiguity in terms like access, authorization and some other terms," Tompkins says. There are also a variety of schemes for intruding in other people's computers that are not covered by the existing statute.

However, law enforcers and legal experts cannot agree on whether the nation needs new laws aimed specifically at combating computer-related crimes or whether the existing laws are adequate.

"New statutes, complete with precise technical definitions, only lead to legal problems," says Ken Citarella.

He advocates "making older statutes fit new crimes," even though he was a member of the state computer crime panel that wrote New York's current computer law.

Computers and the information they contain should be considered property, and like any other property, would be covered under existing statutes, he argues: "If a vandal breaks into a computer, why would that be any different than if he breaks into a car?"

"I see it the other way around," Tompkins says. "Without specific legislation that deals with current technology, you have to rely on old theories of law covering trespass and embezzlement, for example, that are difficult to apply to current computer crimes. It is easier to attack the law generally than for someone to attack it specifically."

A Lack of Computer Ethics

The nation's laws governing computer crimes are strong, but its ethics concerning the use of computer technology are weak, according to Larry Potts, chief of the white-collar crimes program at the Federal Bureau of Investigation.

Computers that are easier to use, their widespread accessibility and the population's growing literacy have "fueled the fire of computer-related crimes," says Potts. Existing laws governing white-collar and computer-related crimes are adequate. "Most computer crimes are traditional crimes; instead of using a knife or gun in the attempt, the criminal uses a computer. What is needed is a reinforcement of ethics."

Too many citizens believe that computer crimes are victimless and that illegally accessing a computer system causes little harm, Potts says. Yet, the same people would never dare to pop the lock off an office door and steal from their manager's desk drawers, he added.

Taking a common sense approach to security will go a long way toward curbing computer crime, Potts says. As an example, he cites an instance in which a computer crime was committed after an employee left critical computer passwords and manuals in a trash receptacle outside of a company's computer room.

Potts says that only by improving computer security can business expect to see a reduction in computer crimes. "Prosecution will never be a solution without computer security," he says. "It's like attacking the drug problem by attacking the supply side without addressing the demand side." Computer crimes are not a technological problem but a people problem, Potts adds.

The Goal of Computer Security

The goal of computer security is to preserve the integrity, confidentiality and availability of information, according to several of the country's top security experts. "The fundamental threats that may keep you from attaining this goal are unauthorized disruption, disclosure, modification, or use of information and information resources, whether deliberate or accidental," says Harry DeMaio, national director, proTech/Information Protection Services at Deloitte & Touche.

Many security experts further categorize those fundamental threats in the following ways:

- Dishonest or disgruntled employees

- Hackers and others outside of the company

- Human errors, omissions and accidents

- Environmental damage

- Electrical and telephone fluctuations or outages

- Natural disaster

- Terrorist attacks and civil disruption

- Viruses, logic bombs and other forms of "vandalware"

Robert Tappan Morris and the Internet Worm

The security of the nation's computer networks has been under intense scrutiny since the evening of November 2, 1988 when Robert T. Morris, then a 23-year-old computer science graduate student and son of one of the U.S. government's top computer scientists, released a worm program on the Internet computer network. The rogue program ran amok, multiplying wildly until it had filled the memories of some 6,000 computers.

The worm program itself did not cause any damage to the systems it attacked in the sense that it did not steal, corrupt, or destroy data and did not alter the systems themselves. However, its uncontrolled multiplication caused computers to slow down to a point of being unusable and in many cases caused computers to shut down completely.

To this day, it is still uncertain what costs were incurred in lost computer resources and the time and manpower needed to clear the worm from infected computer systems. At the very minimum, the costs amounted to well over $250,000, based on the most conservative estimates.

Morris, suspended from Cornell University following the incident, was indicted in July 1989 on a single felony count under the Computer Fraud and Abuse Act of 1986. He was sentenced to three years probation and a $10,000 fine in May 1990.

The young man said at his trial that he wanted to demonstrate that security procedures at computer installations on Internet were too lax. Morris succeeded and failed at the same time to prove his point.

"Poor security practices contributed to the spread of the [worm] on Internet, and those practices are still there," says Eliot Sohmer, former chief of the Office of Standards and Commercial Product Evaluation at the National Computer Security Center. The center is a branch of the super-secret National Security Agency that focuses on computer security. "Everyone wants total access, but there has to be a balance between ease of operation and reasonable control," he says.

Internet systems managers, especially at universities, hesitate to adopt stricter security measures for fear that their systems will become too unwieldy or difficult for end users, says Eugene Spafford, an assistant professor in the department of computer science at Purdue University.

"The problem with security is not the network itself," Spafford says. "What's needed is a heightened awareness of what security is all about at the individual sites."

Computer hackers from all over the world continue to cruise the Internet — an international computer network that links a wide range of computer systems operated by the U.S. military, defense contractors and academic computer centers, among other organizations here and abroad.

There are some 300,000 sites on Internet, and the network is growing 20% per month, according to a spokesman for the U.S. Department of Defense's Computer Emergency Response Team based at Carnegie Mellon University in Pittsburgh.

The number of attacks on computers via the Internet has increased dramatically within the past year, according to security experts and systems administrators whose computers are linked to the network.

"We see attacks from England, Australia, Spain, Norway . . . There is an incredible number of countries involved," says Eugene Schultz, a computer scientist who heads the Department of Energy's Computer Incidence Advisory Capability at Lawrence Livermore National Laboratory. "There are hacking clubs in every country in Europe."

Some hackers route telephone calls through the Netherlands in order to cover their tracks or because there are no Dutch laws prohibiting illegal computer access. "A lot of the calls are traced back to the Netherlands because it is a free stomping ground," explains Ron Tencati, National Aeronautics and Space Administration Science Internet security manager at Goddard Space Flight Center in Greenbelt, Md.

During the past year, overseas hackers have entered a wide range of sites including Anniston Army Depot in Alabama, Aberdeen Ballistic Research Laboratory in Maryland and the Johnson Space Center in Texas.

An unidentified group of hackers, perhaps Dutch, managed to penetrate about a dozen machines at the University of Chicago in the summer of 1990, says Scott Teissler, vice provost for information technology. In one instance, they deposited word processing files of "government origin" on a machine belonging to a vacationing professor, Teissler says. The pirated files had no apparent value, he added.

"They did no damage, and although they were using accounts illegally, they were using them to explore and probe for access to other machines," Teissler says.

New Technology Brings New Security Risks

Corporate America is embracing technology as never before, putting personal computers into the hands of every white-collar worker and stitching computer systems into international networks.

Yet many information systems security experts fear that what may be good for business may be even better for computer outlaws and make it easier for them to commit new sorts of crimes.

Although technology has made many corporations more competitive, it has also made them more vulnerable to attack from employees and outsiders, says Dan White, partner and regional director of Information Security Services at Ernst & Young.

The rapid adoption of distributed systems, electronic data interchange (EDI), local-area networks and other technology has outpaced the capacity of most companies to secure them against attack, White says.

Telecommunications networks, especially those that cross international boundaries, are also more vulnerable to electronic industrial espionage, according to Noel Matchett, president of Information Security, Inc., a security consulting firm based in Silver Spring, Md.

"Every time valuable information is transmitted on unprotected circuits, there is the possibility it is being intercepted by competitors," Matchett says. "Frequently, transmissions are routed over satellite, microwave and even cellular phone circuits, making theft of information undetectable."

Networks of all types, not just for computers, have proliferated out of control, creating "a lot of security problems" and augmenting the number of potential points of unauthorized entry into company computer systems, White says. "The networks are without end points, and most IS managers do not even know how extensive their networks really are," he added.

Many foreign competitors are also being aided by their nations' intelligence organizations in carrying out this electronic eavesdropping, according to Matchett, who previously worked for the National Security Agency on communication security issues. "They are actively participating in it; there is even tasking for certain information for their countries' businesses."

Calculating losses as a result of electronic industrial espionage is a difficult task because unauthorized access to databases is rarely discovered and there is no immediate evidence of theft, he says. However, Matchett says he believes that the losses may reach into the billions of dollars per year.

Investigating and prosecuting crimes that cross national, legal and cultural boundaries will also be difficult, if not impossible, says Raymond Humphrey, director of corporate security at Digital Equipment Corp. "There are no walls around a hacker, who can conceivably start his or her activity in Australia and leap across national boundaries to the U.S.," Humphrey says.

Although computer hackers and others may become more adept at penetrating corporate computer systems, the majority of computer-related crimes will still be carried out by insiders, according to most security experts. If anything, insider attacks will increase, they say.

"The 16- to 17-year-old hacker of a few years ago is now an adult looking for a job and is getting hired," says John Venezia, a data security investigator at Electronic Data Systems Corp. Professional hackers working inside a corporation are able to identify weaknesses that outsiders could never expect to uncover, he says.

Adding to the problem is the fact that end users are becoming increasingly computer-literate, and few firms are laying down ground rules that regulate employee access to company systems from home or elsewhere.

"The problems are caused by nontechnical people making mistakes and insiders manipulating data for their personal benefit," says Robert Courtney, an independent computer security consultant. "The dollar damage by hackers compared to that caused by insiders is nothing." He disagreed with the notion that corporate computer systems are becoming more vulnerable: "The way we're designing computer systems does not create any more opportunity," he adds.

Attacks On Military Systems

Dutch hackers ransacked U.S. Department of Defense computers at 34 sites in April and May of 1991, in some cases modifying or copying information linked to military operations in the Persian Gulf War, according to an official at the General Accounting Office (GAO).

At many of the sites, the hackers were able to access sensitive, nonclassified information related to the transport of military personnel, equipment and weapons systems development data, says Jack Brock, Jr., a GAO director, in testimony in November 1991 before the Senate Subcommittee on Government Information and Regulation.

Personnel information could be used to target employees who may be willing to sell classified information, Brock says. "Further, some DoD and government officials have expressed concern that the aggregation of unclassified, sensitive information could result in the compromise of classified information," he added.

U.S. troops in the Middle East were not jeopardized by the theft of DoD information, but the GAO's findings indicate a "potentially serious threat to our national security," says Sen. Herb Kohl (D-Wis.).

The hackers were able to weave their way across the Internet network through university, government and commercial computers, using those systems to carom into military computers, Brock notes.

The hackers broke into the systems by exploiting widely known loopholes such as default passwords and flaws in computer operating system software. In many of the intrusions, the hackers modified systems to obtain system administrator privileges and created privileged accounts.

"It appears that we were lucky this time," Kohl notes in a prepared statement.

The intrusions highlight how little attention U.S. government agencies give to computer security despite passage of the Computer Security Act of 1987, Congressman Dan Glickman (D-Kan.) told the subcommittee. Glickman authored the act.

"Despite the obvious threat, our own agencies are simply thumbing their noses at this law," Glickman says.

The security statute's intent is to improve the security and privacy of sensitive information in federal computers by establishing minimum security practices. The act, in part, requires agencies to identify computers with sensitive information and develop a security plan for them.

The GAO reported in May 1990 that none of the agencies had fully implemented planned security controls, and only 38% of the 145 security plans had been put into place.

According to agency officials, budget constraints and inadequate top management support — in terms of resources and commitment — were key reasons that controls had not been implemented.

Foreign hackers have been able to freely penetrate a wide range of U.S. government computer systems in recent years. For example, Israeli officials say in September an 18-year-old hacker had penetrated computers at the Pentagon and retrieved classified information related to the Patriot missile and other military secrets during the Persian Gulf War.

Also, a 20-year-old computer science student in Australia is awaiting trial on charges of allegedly hacking into U.S. government, university, and commercial computers in February and March 1990. Prosecutors allege that the student shut down a NASA computer for 24 hours and destroyed computer files belonging to a Texas corporation, among other crimes.

Industrial Strength Computer Hacking

Glasnost may have occasioned a thaw in East-West relations, but many of the spies who have come in from the cold are as busy as ever. Instead of spying on each other, however, foreign intelligence agencies are focusing on industrial espionage, with U.S. computer systems as one of the prime targets, according to several security experts who warn much of that data lies unprotected.

"Industrial espionage is highly profitable," according to Stanislav Levchenko, a former director of Soviet KGB covert activities in the Far East who defected to the U.S. in 1979. He adds that Russia, increasingly strapped for hard currency as well as technology, will boost its industrial espionage efforts "manyfold from what it was a few years ago."

Harry B. Brandon, the FBI's deputy assistant director for intelligence, agrees with that assessment. He says in 1991 Eastern European countries substantially cut back on espionage activities against the U.S., but that the former Soviets have not. In particular, the former Soviets have stepped up efforts to steal economic and technical information, he says.

Former foes are not the only worry, however. Longtime allies are also prying into U.S. technological interests. In November 1990, W. Douglas Gow, a Federal Bureau of Investigation assistant director who heads foreign counterintelligence operations, confirmed reports in a television interview that France's general director of exterior security tried to hire employees in the European offices of IBM, Texas Instruments, Inc., and other U.S. electronics companies to provide information for pay.

The French agency was attempting to gather research and marketing information for Compagnie des Machines Bull, which is owned primarily by the French government. The scheme, which took place in 1987 and 1988, was uncovered by the Central Intelligence Agency and the FBI, Gow says.

"Corporate America doesn't believe people listen to their telephone calls"

The company viewed the incident as a "government-to-government thing" and refused to comment further on the snooping charge, according to a TI spokesman. The company also declined to talk about information security at any level, citing "internal reasons" and concern that it might encourage snooping by outsiders.

Such reluctance to comment on industrial spying is typical, says Dick Heffernan, president of R.J. Heffernan Associates, Inc., an information security firm in Branford, Conn. Heffernan is also chairman of the American Society for Industrial Security's Committee on Safeguarding Proprietary Information.

"Most companies do not want to talk about loss of information because people will think their competitive position has been damaged, and they don't want the value of their stock eroded," Heffernan says.

As more U.S. corporations expand their businesses worldwide, the problem of information theft by professional snoops will likely worsen, Heffernan says. The awareness of this potential risk is "not at a level we are pleased with," he added.

Industrial spying by foreign intelligence agencies, often at the request of their domestic corporations, is the tip of the iceberg, according to Stephen Bryen, president of Deltatech Corp. in Silverspring, Md., and a former deputy undersecretary of defense for trade policy. Industrial espionage by foreign intelligence agencies is increasing and aimed squarely at U.S. computer and electronics industries, Bryen and other experts say. "Clearly the Western Europeans and Japanese have made up their minds where the real competition with us will take place."

Some in Congress say the CIA and the National Security Agency should match the industrial intelligence-gathering activities of U.S. allies such as France, Britain and Japan, which have traditionally shared intelligence data with industry. For example, in the hearings on the nomination of Robert Gates to head the CIA, Gates came under pressure to commit to a similar linkage with American industry.

What can U.S. firms do to protect themselves from industrial espionage? Most experts say the single greatest mistake managers make is failing to take the threat seriously.

"Corporate America doesn't believe people listen to their telephone calls," says Howard M. Ferrill, president of the Operations Security Professionals Society. He cites an FBI estimate that 90% of all voice and fax transmissions going overseas are intercepted by one or more foreign intelligence agencies.

Another common mistake is giving information security duties to the Information Systems (IS) manager, who may lack the needed skills, job description and compensation program to improve security.

Few companies are even aware that this sort of electronic eavesdropping is going on and are skeptical when alerted to possible security breaches, says Thomas Sobczak, vice president of Application Configured Computers, Inc., a security consulting and software publishing company in Baldwin, N.Y. The three-employee company also maintains a database of classified and sensitive information that has leaked out of federal agencies and large corporations.

Electronic Eavesdropping

It apparently does not take the skills of James Bond to be an effective electronic snooper. In the mid-1980s, Winn Van Eck, a Dutch engineer, proved how easy it is to pick up electromagnetic emissions from computers and peripherals by aiming a homemade electronic interception system at the Amsterdam Postal, Telegram & Telegraph office and tapping into its computers.

A "Van Eck listener," as the eavesdropping device is sometimes called, is effective up to several hundred yards and can be made "for $400 max," according to Ian Murphy, founder of IAM/Secure Data Systems, Inc., a Philadelphia-based security consulting firm.

Computers and communications networks are "wide open" to electronic eavesdropping, says Glenn Whidden, who served in the CIA for 28 years and is now a principal at Technical Services Agency, Inc. in Fort Washington, Md. His firm designs and markets equipment for detecting illicit listening devices. A telephone tapping device that is virtually impossible to detect can be assembled from $25 worth of parts from Radio Shack, Whidden says.

"Intercepting a fax is a piece of cake; microwaves and satellite transmissions are free for the taking," says Stephen Bryen. Wireless local-area networks based on infrared or spread-spectrum radio technologies, which have been introduced in recent years, may also be vulnerable to electronic snooping.

Tracking a Wily Hacker in The Cuckoo's Egg

For more than a year, a hacker broke into hundreds of computer systems, stole sensitive, defense-related information and sold it to the KGB for money and drugs until Clifford Stoll spotted his tracks and nailed him.

The Cuckoo's Egg, Stoll's account of his efforts to track a spy through a web of international computer networks, is a fascinating year-long journey that culminates in the arrest of a band of West German computer hackers turned agents of the KGB.

The story begins in 1986, on Stoll's second day of work as a systems manager at Lawrence Berkeley Laboratory in California. Stoll, an astronomer by training, became a computer security expert by accident after his grant money ran out and he was transferred to the computer center in the building where he worked at the University of California at Berkeley.

As the "new kid on the block," says Stoll, he was given the task of trying to resolve an inexplicable 75-cent accounting error. Stoll's first thought is that the error was probably caused by someone using a "few seconds of computing time without paying for it." However, it turned out to be the hacker's first unauthorized excursion into the system.

This was no ordinary hacker, merely interested in cracking passwords and breaking into computer systems for the challenge. The hacker methodically broke into some 400 computers connected to Internet, the nationwide scientific and defense research network, by ingeniously exploiting little-known bugs in Unix software. Once inside the systems, he left behind "cuckoo's egg programs," which, when hatched by the operating system, would give him super user status.

"The cuckoo lays her eggs in other birds' nests," Stoll explains. "She is a nesting parasite: Some other bird will raise her young. Our mysterious visitor laid an egg program into our computer, letting the system hatch it and feed it privileges."

It quickly became evident to Stoll that the hacker was after data about nuclear weapons, the Strategic Defense Initiative, intelligence satellites and other information that was potentially damaging to national security if it found its way into the wrong hands.

Instead of simply locking out the intruder, however, Stoll jury-rigged a battery of outmoded and little-used teletypes, printers and portable computers to record the intruder's every keystroke. The hacker was allowed to roam the system at will in hopes that he would stay on-line long enough for Stoll to arrange for a telephone trace.

To keep the intruder prowling the systems, Stoll contrived dozens of files laced with bogus secret documents that the hacker would spend hours reading and copying.

Once it became clear that the hacker was out to steal information that may be vital to the nation's defense, Stoll attempted to interest the Federal Bureau of Investigation, the Central Intelligence Agency and other federal government agencies in the case.

However, his many initial attempts to enlist their aid were rebuffed, in part because it was not clear to the bureaucrats that the hacker had actually committed a crime and later, when it was determined that the hacker was operating out of Europe, whether they had any jurisdiction in the case.

Eventually the federal government, in cooperation with the Hanover police, closed in and arrested the hacker, who turned out to be a member of a small band of hackers who sold their computer secrets to the KGB for cocaine and thousands of dollars.

Computer Viruses: A Growing Epidemic

Computer viruses, which can wipe out valuable data in less time than it takes to read this sentence, have reached epidemic proportions in only a few years. What's more, the epidemic and the costs of coping with the problem are bound to get worse, according to several computer security experts.

A virus is computer code that replicates and inserts itself into a program and runs when the program is executed. Unlike a computer worm, another form of "vandalware" that also reproduces, a virus is not a distinct program and cannot run by itself. The harm that viruses may do ranges from causing a message to pop up unexpectedly on a user's computer screen to the complete and irretrievable loss of data and programs stored on a hard disk.

The latest count of PC viruses is about 1,200, according to John McAfee, president of McAfee Associates and chairman of the Computer Virus Industry Association in Santa Clara, Calif.

Viruses that attack Apple Computer, Inc., Macintoshes number about 10 and are beginning to multiply rapidly, according to the virus busters.

"It is the single biggest security exposure outside of users making errors," says William Hugh Murray, an information systems security consultant in Wilton, Conn.

The rate at which new viruses are being discovered is accelerating, and with corporate America's increased reliance on local- and wide-area networks, viruses also are spreading faster than ever, security experts says.

Even if no new viruses are created, the cost to the worldwide microcomputing community is likely to exceed $1.5 billion simply to periodically remove malicious software, according to Peter Tippett, President of Foundationware, Inc., a Cleveland-based publisher of anti-virus software.

"The potential costs involved in lost data, system downtime and recovery efforts are likely to exceed $5 billion to $10 billion dollars in the next five years," Tippett says.

Calculating the cost of eradicating and recovering from computer viruses may be nearly impossible, argues Harold Highland, an expert on computer viruses and a former editor of the *Computer Virus Handbook*.

"You can put any price tag on it you want," Highland says. Figures such as Tippett's are based on assumptions that companies are not going to take better precautions to prevent virus attacks or that computer technology will stand still, he says.

Computer viruses of the future will be more professionally written and more destructive than they are now

---

"Firms are not going to continue with business as usual," Highland says. Corporate America is "very concerned about viruses and [is] getting to the point where [it] will adopt specific security measures" to ward them off. Companies "are going to have to make the assumption they are going to get hit sooner than later if only from employee carelessness," Highland says. "The question you have to ask is: 'What do I have to spend to clean up quickly?'"

Highland advocates that large corporations be willing to employ "two top-notch micro people" who are charged with educating users about sound computer practices, scanning all software that is brought into the company and cleaning up virus outbreaks whenever they occur.

The SWAT team and hardware would cost between $120,000 and $150,000 per year, he estimated. "[Firms] are going to have to accept it as a cost of doing business in the same way a retail store factors in the cost of shoplifting," he says.

The alternative is to buy different anti-virus programs at $5 to $50 apiece per machine, which would have to be replaced every few weeks as new viruses are introduced, he says.

Most damage is caused not by viruses but by naive computer users trying to rid their PCs of viruses after being hit, says David Stang, director of research at the National Computer Security Association in Washington, D.C.

"The advice we have had so far is to wait until you see it and then purge it," Murray says. "That is no longer the conservative approach. We ought to immunize every machine."

Katie Hogue, president of Media Markets, Inc. in Alexandria, Va., clearly agrees. She has yet to recover from having two PCs at her firm hit with the 4096 virus. This virus, which appeared after the computers were upgraded at a local computer store, infected some 220 files on floppy and hard disks. "All of my disks were infected, and because I never made backup copies of my masters, we lost all of our programs," Hogue says.

The cost of replacing programs and disks and hiring technicians to eradicate the virus amounted to $4,000. It may be impossible to calculate the cost of not being able to use the two computers for a month. "It would have been cheaper to buy new PCs," Hogue says.

The 4096 is one of a new generation of highly destructive "Stealth" viruses, first spotted in the U.S. nearly a year ago, that appear to be spreading faster than previous generations of the techno-diseases. They are called Stealth viruses because they have been designed by their authors to avoid detection by anti-virus software, much as a Stealth bomber avoids radar.

They are difficult to remove even when found. The Stealth viruses, which include the 4096, Fish, Dark Avenger, and Joshi, are highly prolific and will often change like chameleons to avoid detection or latch onto files as they are being scanned by anti-virus software.

The problems caused by viruses are expected to continue to escalate, according to several experts. "The volcano is rumbling, but no one is paying attention," says A. Padgett Peterson, a member of the professional staff and a computer virus expert at Martin Marietta Missiles and Electronics Group, a division of Martin Marietta Corp. in Orlando, Fla. Computer viruses of the future will be more professionally written and more destructive than they are now, he says.

Of immediate concern is a lack of anti-virus software that adequately protects local-area networks, Peterson says. He is responsible for protecting, among other systems, more than 5,000 personal computers and 200 minicomputers at Martin Marietta.

Peterson says that no single anti-virus software package can do an adequate job of protecting computer systems. He advocates using two or three anti-virus products that regularly scan for malicious code as well as sound an alarm whenever a file has been inexplicably altered.

Even with the best precautions, computer viruses continue to infiltrate the company's systems. Not long ago, three-quarters of the 2,000 PCs on a LAN were knocked out by a virus, Peterson says.

Terrorists Plug into Information Age

Major corporations will also have to contend with attacks on their computer systems, data centers and networks by terrorists, special-interest groups and politically-minded hackers.

Attacks on computer systems already account for some 60% of all terrorist attacks in the world, says Martin Cetron, president of Forecasting International Ltd., a consulting firm based in Arlington, Va. In an article published in *The Futurist* magazine in 1989, Cetron said 24 computer centers were bombed in West Germany in one year. Italy's Red Brigades and France's Action Directe have also targeted computer systems in Europe. "It is only a matter of time before someone takes advantage of U.S. computer vulnerability," he says.

"It seems as though terrorists are tuning into the information age," says Steve Sawyer, co-founder of SG Systems, Inc., an anti-virus software publisher in San Francisco and co-host of a forum on "The Well," a popular electronic bulletin board. "It is like planting a bomb," he says. "Although it is bloodless, it may have even more of an impact."

Security experts say they believe that special-interest groups out to stymie corporations whose businesses are thought to have a deleterious effect on the environment, for instance, will begin making computer systems the targets of their protests. "Instead of spiking trees, they are going to spike computer systems," Sawyer says.

With the widespread dependence on computer systems by industry and government, it won't be long before terrorists put computer systems in their sights, concurs Winn Schwartau, executive director of Inter Pact, a consulting company in Nashville, Tenn. The well-armed terrorist has an arsenal of at least seven types of weapons to use against computers, Schwartau says.

According to Schwartau, these weapons include:

❑ **Viruses and Worms** — As of June 1991, there were approximately 900-1,000 viruses on the loose. Schwartau estimates that 15 to 18 news viruses are created each day. "At that rate there will be 100,000 viruses by 1995," he says. It won't be long before terrorists set up "virus factories" to mass produce viruses designed to cause mayhem and mistrust among computer users, he says.

Already, computer viruses and worms carrying political messages are popping up with alarming frequency. For example, the Fu Manchu virus discovered in 1988 in the UK sought out the names of certain politicians—such as Thatcher, Reagan and Botha—in word processing files and tacked on rude remarks about these political figures.

The worm known as Worms Against Nuclear Killers, or WANK, which was twice pumped into the National Aeronautics and Space Administration's largest space and earth science network in 1989 and 1990, is believed to have been a protest against the launch of a space shuttle that was carrying a nuclear-powered space probe.

❑ **Sniffers** — Off-the-shelf software, intended to analyze local-area networks, can be used to eavesdrop on communications and collect passwords. "These are tools that can be used against us," Schwartau says.

❑ **Electromagnetic Eavesdropping** — Computer monitors, printers, keyboards and wires emanate data in the form of electromagnetic radiation. Using a device such as a Van Eck antenna, that radiation and the accompanying data can easily be intercepted. "Finding the PIN (personal identification number) of an ATM (automatic teller machine) user is trivial," Schwartau says.

❑ **HERF Guns** — A high energy pulse shot from a High Energy Radio Frequency (HERF) gun into a computer system or network could force a glitch or crash the system, he says. Repeatedly shooting a system with such a device could cause incalculable difficulties for the target.

❑ **EMP/T Bombs** — If the HERF signal is amplified sufficiently, a short burst of energy would be enough to cause transistors and other electronics to explode, wipe out data on memory chips and disks, and cause other damage. A small EMP/T (electromagnetic pulse transformer) bomb could wipe out every computer inside buildings for blocks, Schwartau claims.

Security Failures Have Management Liability

In March 1989, an oil tanker ripped open its hull on a reef, gushing millions of gallons of black crude into Alaska's Prince William Sound. The ship's captain, alleged to have been napping in his bunk, faced criminal charges in the aftermath of the spill.

There are lessons to be learned from the Alaskan disaster that corporate executives would do well to heed lest, like the captain of the grounded tanker, they be hauled into court, according to several computer security professionals and legal experts. The charge? Failure to adequately protect their corporate computer systems against hacker attacks, viruses and other serious breaches of security.

"Corporate and governmental computer systems are like the Exxon Valdez— unprotected, under inadequate leadership control, operating through dangerous channels and loaded with valuable and messy stuff," says Sanford Sherizen, president of Data Security Systems, Inc., a computer-crime prevention firm based in Natick, Mass.

"Corporate exposure and vulnerability has outstripped the rate of acceptance and proliferation of computer systems and networks," agrees Kenneth Weiss, chief technical officer at Security Dynamics, Inc. and chairman of the computer security division of the American Defense Preparedness Association. "If [senior management] really understood the potential liability and the potential risks to corporate assets and to their reputations, they might shut down all networks and computer centers."

Although there are few absolute IS security standards now in place, "we are moving to an era of mandatory data security," Sherizen says. "Computer crime laws and regulatory requirements, new auditing perspectives, insurability definitions, public relations liabilities and due-care considerations all contribute to this trend," Sherizen added.

Several experts agree that the prospect of a serious computer security breach — one causing a company to go bankrupt or harming its employees or customers in some other way — is likely to increase. Distributed information systems and the networks that interconnect them have made corporations more competitive, but at the same time they have made them more vulnerable to attack by disgruntled employees, hackers and others, they note.

As computer systems are pushed out to end users, the responsibility for securing those systems is also distributed. That responsibility is not necessarily understood or readily accepted by end users, the experts say.

In the event of a computer-security breach that harms an individual or corporation, senior managers, officers and directors are someday going to be held responsible, he says.

According to Randall Miller, executive vice-president and general counsel at Compusource Corp., which markets disaster recovery services through its Hotsite division, a vice-president or manager of IS can be held personally liable for a catastrophic loss because of a data processing disaster if there are actions that he or she could have taken to prevent the loss but did not.

There have been numerous court cases in which disgruntled shareholders sued officers, directors and agents for alleged wrongdoing, he says. From these cases has come a standard called the "prudent man rule" that requires officers and others to discharge their duties with the due diligence and care that ordinary, prudent people would exercise under similar circumstances.

However, there are no generally accepted standards of due care for the protection of computerized data, says Michael Agranoff, a Stafford Springs, Conn. attorney who specializes in computer law. "What this means in practical terms is that industry does not need to provide meaningful computer security, since it will almost certainly not be liable to persons injured as a result of unauthorized access to computerized data," he says.

Mandatory minimum standards for computer security are inevitable, according to Agranoff and several other experts. The issue is whether those standards will be adopted voluntarily by corporations or foisted upon them by force of law.

A handful of states — Florida and California, for example — have recently passed legislation that would require state agencies to take measures to adequately protect their computer systems.

Some states also require insurance carriers to adhere to certain security guidelines, but the standards are not uniform and definitions vary widely.

The Computer Security Act of 1987 mandates that federal agencies take adequate steps to secure their computer systems and calls for the National Institute of Standards and Technology (NIST), with assistance from a 12-member panel, to develop computer security guidelines. However, arguments between NIST and the National Security Agency over who has authority to establish computer security guidelines has stymied efforts to comply with the act, Agranoff added.

"The idea is that such standards and guidelines would permeate to the private sector, as Cobol standards did over 20 years ago," Agranoff says. Industry needs the equivalent of the Department of Defense's trusted computer systems criteria, the so-called Orange Book, according to Willis Ware, a corporate research staffer at Rand Corp.

FYI: A Short Dictionary of Vandalware

Virus: A virus is a piece of code that operates only when its host programs run. Once it executes, the virus often copies itself into a program and replicates to infect other programs. They behave in a wide variety of ways, ranging from popping up a simple message on screen to destroying data.

Worm: Unlike a virus, a worm is able to execute independently; in other words, it is a complete, functional program. It reproduces and travels from one computer to another, typically over a network. Generally, worms do not modify programs or data. However, that does not mean it is benign. A worm may multiply rapidly, causing a computer to shutdown and in that process cause data to be lost.

Trojan Horse: Like the fabled wooden horse in Greek mythology, a Trojan horse is more than what it first appears to be. In computer software, a Trojan horse hides in a program that is often appealing. When the attractive program runs, a hidden program also goes into action, often behaving in unexpected or unwanted ways. In many cases, it grabs passwords, which the Trojan's author can use to break into a system.

Bomb: There are two types of bombs: logic and time. Both are a type of Trojan horse that is used to release a virus or other form of vandalware. A logic bomb triggers when certain conditions are met, such as when software is used, perhaps without paying for it, a specific number of times. A time bomb triggers on a specific date, such as Friday the 13th.

Trap Door: Software designers, and sometimes clever hackers, leave electronic holes in computer software that allows them to circumvent normal security procedures. The trap door may be there to allow the software designer to test the system; other times, a hacker will leave a trap door to secretly enter a system.

Chapter 8:

Current Solutions to Computer Security Problems

"Protecting information is *not* natural. On the contrary, it runs counter to many of our deepest urges — intellectual curiosity, the need to communicate, the need to socialize, to trust and be trusted. In fact, we are usually suspicious of people or institutions that are secretive, regardless of their reasons. Nor are we consistent. While carefully trying to protect our own privacy, most of us are still fascinated by other people's scandals."

— From "Information Protection and Other Unnatural Acts," by Harry DeMaio, National Director, proTech/Information Protection Services at Deloitte & Touche.

Protecting corporate computer systems from a disgruntled employee from within or from a 16-year old hacker from outside is easy. Merely take all computers, disconnect them from any network, lock them in a windowless, lead-lined room and throw away the key. Then post a guard at the door.

That obviously is not a solution that will appeal to many computer users, perhaps with the exception of military personnel who handle classified data. However, it is the only approach to certain security.

Although a completely fail-safe system is not yet available, companies can implement security systems using a combination of products and methods that will discourage most types of security breaches.

Experts say that many security breaches succeed because the obvious physical security procedures have been overlooked and not from the result of sophisticated electronic theft.

Taking such precautions as locking doors, restricting access to personal computers and workstations and properly disposing of materials that may provide clues to the inner workings of a company's computer operations are an effective first line of defense, the experts say.

Intruders are often deterred by the simple knowledge that security procedures have been implemented and that computer users are trained to spot most irregularities. However, for those who are not likely to be put off from attempting to break into a company system, preventive measures should be in place to bar attempts at unauthorized access.

If protective measures fail, the system should at least issue a warning to appropriate personnel that a security breach has occurred and it should produce an audit trail so that information systems administrators can trace its origin.

Most computer crime— whether it is the unauthorized access to a company's files or the planting of a time bomb designed to destroy programs and data — is likely to be carried out by current or former employees.

The trick is to enable computer users to make the most of systems while at the same time making some reasonable attempt to protect company data. If the guidelines are overly stringent, end users cannot do their work effectively. On the other hand, if they are too loose, there's the risk of a disgruntled employee bollixing up data.

Controlling Access to Computer Systems

"The main aim of a security program is to allow authorized persons and processes to do what they are supposed to do and to prevent everything else," says Harry DeMaio, a security expert and national director, proTech/Information Protection Services at Deloitte & Touche. "The shorthand term is access control."

There are basically four types of access controls:

- System access controls, for example, passwords;

- data access controls, in which the system controls what information people can read and not read or tamper with in any way;

- system and security administration, such as computer user security training; and

- system design, taking advantage of basic hardware and software security features.

Data security does not have to be an all or nothing proposition. Analysts suggest for a typical company only about 5% to 10% of the data needs to be protected. In fact, protecting up to 80% of company data would use up only 20% of a security budget; it is the final 20% of data that would be most costly to protect, the experts say.

For a typical company different levels of security should be used. The highest level of security should be provided to mission critical and sensitive information such as strategic plans and proprietary information. A medium level of security is recommended for proprietary information, such as company finances and product plans. Lowest security considerations should be accorded confidential information such as payroll, personnel or medical records.

Authenticating Users

There are only three basic ways to identify a person at a terminal:

❑ something he knows, such as password;

❏ something he has, such as a card with a magnetic stripe; and

❏ something he is, such as a fingerprint.

Passwords

Passwords are one of the oldest ways to limit who can use a computer system. The idea is that if you know the secret password for an account, you must be the rightful user of that account. The problem of course, is that passwords can be stolen or easily figured out. Some password software programs aim to overcome this limitation by randomly generating passwords that are difficult to crack or by regularly prompting users and systems administrators to change their passwords.

Poorly chosen passwords and failure to change the default passwords often included with new hardware and software remain the primary security loopholes, according to experts.

"The biggest shortcoming is still the way they do password administration and management," says Peter Goldis, a computer security expert. "One thing big corporations should do better is stress the importance of password security, password selection and the dangers of password sharing."

In any case, using passwords to limit access to computer systems is gradually falling out of favor in Corporate America.

America is on the brink of "an electronic Pearl Harbor," declares Scott Chasin, a former hacker and one of the founders of Comsec Data Security, Inc., a Houston, Texas-based security consulting firm. "A lot of things that companies, especially the Fortune 500, are doing such as changing the passwords every month, requiring a punctuation mark or numeric character in a password is not going to cut it."

A Primer on Choosing Passwords

There are bound to be systems for which the usual password protections will be adequate. Some suggestions from noted security expert, Harold Highland follow:

◆ Set a minimum of characters (at least eight) for a password to keep users from creating simple two-, three- and four-character passwords that are easy to divine.

◆ Pick a word in English and then use a foreign translation culled from a translation dictionary.

◆ Use a password phrase instead of a one-word password.

◆ Use a combination of lower and upper case letters and numbers in a password.

Password Alternatives

Are memorized computer security passwords passé? Quite a few computer scientists and security experts believe so.

"I predict that within five years, most systems will have a higher level of security beyond simple password protection than exists today," says Doug McIlroy, one of Bell Laboratories' top computer scientists. He envisions that computer systems will be protected by some form of password calculating device — mainly, a combination of decoder box and key.

Devices such as "tokens" and "smart cards," which are designed to generate new passwords every time they are used, are slowly becoming popular as alternatives to traditional password management methods.

The first of these devices is a plain credit card with a magnetic stripe; the second is a smart card, about the same dimensions of a credit card but with a built-in microprocessor that stores passwords and other data; and the third is a token, which typically looks like a pocket calculator, complete with buttons and liquid crystal display. It is also about the same size as a credit card. Of the three, tokens are getting the closest looking over by corporate America.

In ancient times, a courier would carry a ring, seal or some other object as proof of his authority to speak for a ruler. Today, a token is used to verify that the computer user is the person he or she claims to be.

With the token system, the user "owns" the token after it has been assigned a personal identification number, like that used to operate an automatic teller machine. The token works in sync with software loaded on any system, from laptops to mainframes. Operating a token-based system is simple: The user enters his log-on identification into the handheld device, the computer responds with a challenge and asks for a password, and the user responds.

Security expert Harold Highland says he prefers this "question-response technique" because the challenge and password change with each access and is virtually foolproof.

Having a password plus a token is the ideal way to create good security, agrees Kenneth Weiss, chairman and chief technical officer of Security Dynamics, Inc., a Cambridge, Mass. firm that markets computer protection devices.

"This is called a two-factor security system," Weiss explains. "For example, your credit card is a two-factor security system. It has on it a relatively difficult-to-counterfeit token, a holograph. Also, consider that many credit cards and other types of identification have three- factor security: they also have a picture of the individual on them. The picture, a signature and the device itself represent three factors. An example of this is a passport."

The token generates and displays a number that is unique to each card and one that varies every time the user accesses a computer — that number plus a password is entered in the system. This makes it look like the computer has been given two passwords. One of them meets the standards of a secret, discreet password that the user knows, and the other one comes off the card, Weiss explains.

"The number that the card displays looks just like a password but it is not," Weiss says. "Rather, it proves that the user has physical possession of the card. The number is unique to the card. Obviously, every time the card is used, a new number is selected pseudo-randomly so that it cannot be predicted. The number off the card identifies that the user possesses a token, namely the card that produced the number. Thus, when it is combined with a password, this system comprises a two-factor security system."

Biometric Technologies

Biometric security devices examine the physical actions or traits that make each individual unique. There are six types of devices currently available and at least two more under development.

They work in a similar manner: A biometric portrait of the subject is scanned or read by sensor devices, converted into digital data and stored. In verification, the subject's handprint, voice or other trait is compared with the stored profile.

- **Retina Scanners** — The back of a person's eyeball contains tiny blood vessels arranged in patterns that are as unique as fingerprints. Retina scanners read the size, location and pattern of blood vessels in the back of the eye.

- **Signature Dynamics** — Forgers can mimic the appearance of a signature, but a biometric pen or pad measures signature dynamics: the pressure exerted by the writer on the pen point and the motion used in writing, for example.

- **Keystroke Analysis** — Keystroke analysis compares the individual patterns and rhythms of typing repetitive character groups.

- **Hand Geometry** — Hand geometry systems measure finger length, skin translucency and palm thickness and shape, among other characteristics.

- **Fingerprint Analysis** — Even junior criminologists know that no two fingerprints are identical. Fingerprint or thumbprint identification systems analyze the unique arches, loops and whorls of a person's finger or thumb.

- **Voice verification** — Voice verification maps the actual physiology that produces speech, not merely sounds or pronunciation.

Under development are two other biometric methods—one that makes use of neural network technology in a device that aims to recognize faces and another that analyzes a person's genetic pattern, or "DNA fingerprint."

Data Encryption

Data encryption programs, often used as a second level of protection, systematically scrambles data to make it unintelligible to unauthorized users but recovers it for authorized users.

There are two types of encryption methods: ciphers and codes. Ciphers scramble individual characters in text; codes manipulate complete words or phrases at a time.

Data can be encoded at a remote workstation communicating to a host computer or a local terminal transmitting a file to a storage device. In order to decipher the code at the receiving point, the operator or device must have the correct decryption code or key.

Encryption devices can be either hardware- or software-based or a combination of both. In the past decade, software applications have become more common, although a number of communications hardware manufacturers now incorporate encryption capabilities in their modem hardware.

Cryptography is the only known practical method to protect information transmitted electronically through communication networks. It can also be an economical way to protect stored data, note researchers at IBM.

Cryptographic methods can be used to protect not only the confidentiality of data, but the integrity of data as well. Data confidentiality is the protection of information from unauthorized disclosure. Data integrity is the protection of information from unauthorized modification.

The largest users of encryption technology are the military and related suppliers and banks and other financial institutions. However, there are many applications today for commercial cryptography. Existing applications provide confidentiality of files and communications, integrity of messages, and user identification.

Communication integrity may be guaranteed by using a message authentication code (MAC) to detect alteration of messages transmitted over networks, IBM explains. The MAC is generated at the message origination node and appended to the message. On receipt of the message and its associated MAC, the MAC is verified at the message destination node.

Another use is the detection of unauthorized file modifications. A modification detection code (MDC) calculation may be used to reduce the problem of maintaining the integrity of data, IBM's researchers note. For example, to detect program alteration, an MDC could be calculated on a known correct version of the program and then published in a generally available forum, such as a newspaper. A recipient of the program can then calculate the MDC for the received program and verify that the resulting MDC is the same. An MDC is different from a MAC in that the formula for calculating an MDC does not use a secret key and is public knowledge.

Encryption should be used all the time on networks, according to Kenneth Weiss. "Encryption equipment today is relatively inexpensive compared to what it was 10 years ago," he says. "Ten years ago you would have needed a $50,000 box at the host, and a $10,000 or $20,000 box at the terminal. Today, you are talking about a $500 to $1,000 device at a terminal and, depending on the channel, some multiple of that at a host."

The drawback to encryption is the requirement for three components that are expensive and in fact insecure: administering a system, generating encryption keys and securely disseminating those keys, Weiss says. "It is in that process that the system falls down. So, an individual may indeed prove to someone who gives him an encryption key that he is authentic, but now you have to be concerned how that key was administered and if copies of that key were given to other people."

Local Area Networks

Corporate America is rushing to "downsize" their computer applications from large mainframe computers to local area networks (LANs) that often link hundreds, and even thousands, of personal computers. At the same time companies may be installing "client/server" architectures, which transfer some computer processing from mainframes to PCs and other computers connected to LANs.

As a result, connecting PCs and other types of computers (usually made by a variety of different manufacturers) has become one of the most pressing security issues facing systems administrators and security managers.

"From a security standpoint, multi-vendor connectivity is a nightmare," says Daniel White, partner and national director of information security at Ernst & Young in Chicago. "PC security is still an oxymoron."

Mainframe security is fairly well established and has been in use for more than three decades. In comparison, LAN security is still in its infancy.

"LAN security right now resembles mainframe security in the '70s," says Thomas Peltier, senior staff assistant, Financial Controls Analysis Section for General Motors Corp. in Detroit. "LAN security features are steadily improving but still do not offer as many features as mainframes."

LANs have 15 points of vulnerability, according to one expert. Those weak points include the user, who may unwittingly disclose his password, to the cables that link computers on the network, which can be tapped.

Security features for network operating systems and applications programs range from file-locking mechanisms to multi-layered security systems. At minimum, most have password facilities. Network applications also usually enable the network manager to control the amount of time a user can access the system and the number of attempts to log onto a system before being shut out.

LAN operating systems, such as Vines, from Banyan Systems, Inc., and NetWare, from Novell, Inc., include basic security features, such as password security, that are executed on a server. These features were adequate five years ago when LANs were only supporting departmental applications, such as word processing and spreadsheets and small numbers of users. With few connections to the outside world, data was pretty much secure.

Today, data travels from LAN to LAN, often spanning hundreds and thousands of miles. The popular LAN operating systems have not been designed to provide security for multiple LANs.

However, users have a variety of options for dealing with current limitations. They can store information on mainframes that require high security. Several software companies are trying to fill the security void. For example, Certus International Corp. and PC Guardian Inc., (among other companies) sell products that enhance LAN security.

Most of these products feature password authentication, access control, audit trails and data encryption and range in price from $400 to $22,000.

Tips to Achieving Local-Area Network Security

A secure networked environment is difficult to achieve but it can be done, according to Kenneth Weiss of Security Dynamics, Inc., in Cambridge, Mass. "It takes a serious approach, advance planning, education and user commitment," he explains. "Servers and personal computers represent the highest security risk on a local area network because their local storage is open to theft."

Here are Weiss's security suggestions for protecting networks:

1). House servers and consoles in the most secure locations. Do not make the mistake of hiding the server behind a cipher lock while the server console is left in an exposed office.

2). Control workstation access by making sure users power down and lock their keyboards when they leave. If operations require greater security, consider removable hard drives.

3). The miles of LAN cabling in many networks are an often overlooked area of vulnerability. Copper cable, particularly twisted pair, can be tapped even without direct wire contact. Fiber cable is much more secure, but not completely.

4).   Many government LANs are using some form of encryption to secure the connections between workstations and servers.

5).   Because personal computers are the weakest link, consider user authentication and file/program security measures for logical access control. Almost every major LAN operating system has basic controls built in to verify users on the basis of controls built in (names) and what they know (passwords).

6).   System administrators should kill passwords frequently and not allow passwords to be names or recognizable words. They should discourage use of the same password on different LANs — if one is compromised, others could follow. Consider a "least-privilege" policy restricting LAN resources on a need-to-know basis.

7).   User privileges should be as restrictive as possible without keeping people from doing their jobs.

8).   Do not forget remote LAN access. If only dial-out service is required, set up modems that do not permit dial-in access. If that is inappropriate, dial-back modems can verify callers' authenticity.

9).   Review all the resources available to authenticated users: servers, disk volumes, directories and files. Most LAN operating systems allow the terminal operator at least to assign read, write and execute privileges. Some can place programs in a directory with file security so users cannot read them.

10). The most sophisticated technology cannot plug all the leaks unless common sense is applied to running the LAN. Impress upon users the need for security. Have an organizational computer security policy that employees must read and agree to as a prerequisite for computer use.

11). Assign a dedicated system manager for each LAN. For large installations, divide the duties between a dedicated system manager and a dedicated information security officer, each having limited capabilities and privileges. That way, a single individual cannot make significant changes to the system.

12). Allow only licensed software on the LAN, and make sure to keep accurate records of vendor addresses, release numbers and license numbers. Preserve the configuration reports in a safe place, in case the software has to be reinstalled later.

13). Finally, impossible as it may sound, set firm guidelines that prohibit users from loading new software onto their machines. Diskless workstations may be the answer.

Mainframe Security: Access Control Software

Mainframe computer security software vendors have greatly improved their mainframe security packages in recent years but the software still does not provide adequate protection for data that is downloaded to personal computers or distributed over networks spanning considerable distances. Somewhat ironically, that view is shared by users and vendors alike.

Three access control packages — Computer Associates ACF2 and Top Secret and IBM's RACF — account for all but a small piece of the market and offer similar capabilities and levels of protection, according to users and security experts.

"All three of the major packages have greatly increased the richness of their facilities," says Peter Goldis, an independent consultant based in Cambridge, Mass., and an expert on IBM mainframe security.

The primary security concern in today's mainframe environment is the proliferation of platforms and networks over wide geographic areas.   Only recently have vendors been able to provide the capability to disperse security through the network and to provide a unified view of the enterprise.

Customers and user groups are asking for enhancements to RACF that will allow them to implement the software over a wider geographic area and to do administrative security chores on a PC, says Rich Guski, senior programmer in RACF design, Kingston, N.Y.

The movement to "openness and interoperability between different kinds of mainframes, so users can hopefully see one homogeneous processing environment," remains an elusive goal, Guski says. "We are looking toward a direction based on the distributed computing environment and how RACF will interplay or interoperate with the administrative function that would be provided within the distributed computing environment."

Hiring a Hacker: Penetration Testing

It is not quite a hacker-for-hire scheme but the idea is the same. Penetration testing — hiring outsiders to probe computer systems for security loopholes — is catching on in corporate America, according to practitioners and some buyers of penetration services.

Penetration testers use many of the same ploys favored by hackers to break into systems, ranging from schmoozing unsuspecting employees in hopes of learning passwords to attempting to log into a system using common passwords.

"There is a market for companies that want the undercover approach because it can be the most revealing," says Peter Goldis, a hacker-for-hire who specializes in electronically attacking computer systems. There is no other way for management to know for certain that what MIS has been saying about its security is indeed true, he says. Goldis has tested computer systems security at more than 25 top corporations in the last three years for fees of $10,000 and higher.

"They may have installed one of the top access-control products — RACF or ACF2 or Top Secret — and they want to know if they overlooked something," Goldis explains. "To test the system, they define a target, create a data set and protect it with all of the mechanisms that are available to them. Then they say to me, if you can update it or even look at it, then we are convinced that we have a problem. It eliminates any ambiguity of what I am setting out to accomplish."

Goldis says that he has never failed to uncover security loopholes in their systems.

When Dennison Manufacturing Co. in Waltham, Mass., hired Goldis to test its computer security, "he opened management's eyes," says Louis Pintsopoulos, who supervises the auditing of electronic data processing at the company.

"I hired him because there was another level of security that needed to be addressed but was too specialized for MIS," Pintsopoulos says. "There are not a lot of people who can do what Peter can do to resolve the problems and also know what the ramifications are."

The services range in cost from $2,000 for a two-day remote test to $30,000 for customized, on-site analysis that could take a week or more.

"We approach it from many different ways, either as an employee who is trying to breach unauthorized access, or as a total outsider who knows nothing about the company, maybe as a computer hacker," says Scott Chasin, one of four founders of Comsec Data Security, Inc., Houston, Texas.

Chasin and two co-founders of Comsec, one of a handful of companies specializing in penetration testing, are self-styled former members of the Legion of

Doom, one of the nation's most notorious hacker groups, according to federal law enforcers.

Chasin claims to have a 100% success rate in breaking into the systems of Comsec's clients. He estimates that the firm could penetrate 80% of the systems in corporate America.

"Once we do penetrate, we try to grab things of value from the system to let (clients) know what somebody could have manipulated, stolen or damaged," Chasin says.

Not all security breaches are carried out electronically, notes Patricia Fisher, president of Janus Associates, Inc., another penetration testing firm based in Stamford, Conn. In one instance, a Janus investigator succeeded in getting a user ID and password simply by sending the client company a letter that said in part Janus was working on a "project" and wanted the company to participate in a "demonstration."

Companies that use penetration testing firms typically have a gamut of security procedures and controls already in place. Penetration testing is a way to make sure the procedures and controls work according to plan, says Peter Davis, an auditor who has used penetration testing firms. He asked not to be further identified.

"It's a different way of assessing the adequacy of the system, and in my mind, a more effective way," Davis says. "They know exactly what to look for."

Battling Computer Viruses and Other Forms of Vandalware

With some 1,200 viruses known to exist, and two to three introduced every day, it is no longer a matter of "if" but "when" a virus will infect a company's PCs, according to the National Computer Security Association (NCSA).

The number of North American companies and government agencies that have been hit with a virus is doubling every 4 to 5 months, according to a recent study commissioned by the association.

Prevention still remains the best approach to coping with viruses. Security experts stress the importance of clear and specific policies that prevent users from inserting diskettes into company computer systems that may be infected with viruses. One survey indicates that the wide majority of virus infections in companies are caused by end users who bring diskettes from home to use.

One way to prevent systems from being infected is to install a virus scanning or detection program on individual PCs. This software automatically checks disks for the presence of specific viruses and will alert users when unexpected or unauthorized activities — such as the increase in the size of a program — occur.

There are at most 20 publishers of anti-virus software that market "scan programs" to detect viruses, "vaccines" that prevent machines from being infected and "antidotes" that help to remove viruses.

The drawback is that anyone of those products is only as good as yesterday's virus, thus requiring end users to regularly update the programs they use to keep ahead of the latest strains.

Some virus experts suspect that viruses are developed and unleashed by companies that also publish anti-virus software, as a way to prime their markets — a charge that has never been substantiated.

The majority of anti-virus products have four or five ways to protect against viruses. Anti-virus software is able to detect unknown or new viruses by monitoring attempts by programs to terminate and stay resident in memory, alter files in inexplicable ways and other techniques.

Despite the risk, less than 20% of companies have installed anti-virus software on their PCs to automatically protect against infection, according to one study.

The lack of interest in anti-virus software can be attributed to the notion that the cure can be nearly as bad as the disease, some end users says.

"Anti-virus software demands perpetual maintenance to be effective," says Albert Belisle, deputy director of corporate information security at The First National Bank of Boston.

Belisle advocates limiting the installation of anti-virus software to high-risk systems that may be used by a wide variety of unsupervised users, and to systems with high strategic value to the company. Elsewhere in the company, "I place heavy emphasis on access control," Belisle says.

"Access control is an obviously reasonable solution," says Robert Jacobson, president of International Security Technology, which markets the Virus-Pro anti-virus package. "The downside is that it creates problems for the user of the PC by adding to the expense, complexity, maintenance, training and so on."

"We would maintain that you should fight a fire with a fire extinguisher, says Tori Case, product manager at Central Point Software, Inc., which markets Central Point Anti-Virus. "Other tools are not specific to viruses."

Promoting Computer Ethics

There are several ways for a company to protect its computer system against intrusion, ranging from setting up audit trails to physically isolating the computer system and limiting access to it. But there is no single solution; nearly all information managers know that it takes a combination of methods to create a fail-safe system.

One measure that companies seldom think about when devising security procedures is the creation of a code of ethics that clearly spells out the company's attitudes about computer security and what the consequences are if an end user violates those procedures.

If an end user duplicates a copyrighted software package, it may not be because he is dishonest; it may be because he is ignorant of the law. This code of conduct can be refined and extended to all end user computing activities, not just to regulation of software copying.

End users need to understand that breaking and entering a computer system is as illegal as popping the lock on the door of a co-worker's office and rummaging through his file cabinets.

"If we find an abuse, we take action,
but we see it as a preventive measure
rather than a corrective one."

"They wouldn't think of going through someone's desk or notebook but think nothing of going through a disk directory," says Ardoth Hassler, assistant director of the Computer Center for Academic Computing at Catholic University of America in Washington, D.C. Catholic University is among several of the nation's academic institutions that has devised a statement of computer ethics.

That statement, which has been in effect for more than eight years, is published in a variety of university publications, including campus newsletters and handbooks for students—the university's primary end users.   "We saw it as an opportunity to provide guidelines for student behavior on computer systems," Hassler says.

"We wanted to devise the statement and the mechanism to educate the user population about what is considered appropriate behavior," Hassler explains. "If we find an abuse, we take action, but we see it as a preventive measure rather than a corrective one."

By itself, a code of ethics will not keep computer systems safe from employees, well meaning or otherwise. Not everyone will follow a code of ethics, just as everyone does not obey the law. But at least you will have spelled out the ground rules and the penalties for end users.

"I would definitely recommend it because it educates rather than punishes users," Hassler points out. "In the event that we do have a problem, it gives us something to stand on, a foundation on which to base your work or punishment."

A Sample Code of Ethics Statement

Here is a sampling of the standards of behavior that are included in the Catholic University's code of ethics:

◆ "Users must not search for, access or copy directories, programs, files, disks or data not belonging to them unless they have specific authorization to do so.

◆ "Users must not attempt to modify the system facilities or attempt to crash the system, nor should they attempt to subvert the restrictions associated with their computer accounts, the networks of which the university is a member or microcomputer software protections.

◆ "Users should make appropriate use of system-provided protection features and take precautions against others obtaining access to their computer resources.

◆ "Users should change their passwords frequently and should avoid using their names, their spouses' or friends' names or a password that could easily be guessed."

Raising Security Awareness

Along with computer ethics, many companies are training end users to be aware of proper computing practices. Videotapes, seminars, posters, articles in company newsletters, and day-long security awareness programs that cover all aspects of security are being used to promote security awareness.

Companies that foster security awareness say that the training must be regular and sustained and a refresher course every six months is not too often. Also, new employees must be trained as soon they are hired in order to impress upon them the importance of security, perhaps before bad habits set in.

Managers must be part of the training equation as well. Managers should be asked to participate in programs and to endorse programs to give them a stamp of legitimacy and importance.

"There is an increased awareness [on the part of managers] of the importance of information to business, even outside security industry circles," says Robert Ferrante, director of data security and systems development at American Express Travel Related Services Co. Also, mounting concerns about consumer privacy and the protection of personal information and general media coverage of security-related issues have been a "big impetus" in boosting security awareness, he says.

Budgets For Security Are Increasing

If there is a positive side to the upsurge of computer crime and abuse in recent years, it is that information systems managers and security professionals plan to increase their computer security budgets.

According to a study published by the Los Angeles-based National Center for Computer Crime Data (NCCCD), expenditures for computer security as a percentage of the overall computer budget have risen about 66% in recent years.

A majority of the 3,500 computer security professionals surveyed report that they plan to step up their purchases of computer security products, most notably anti-virus software. Only 22% planned to buy anti-virus products in 1988, but 54% says they planned to purchase those products during the following two years.

> *"In banking, for example, in five robberies, the robbers will get only $10,000. But in a case of computer fraud, a single robbery may net 20 times as much."*

The respondents say their use of such technologies as smart cards, audit analysis aids, secure networks and encryption systems also will rise dramatically.

Management has to be sold a multifaceted security plan that offers a range of strategies rather than one that stresses some methods over others, says Ken Shaurette, system security administrator at Foremost Life Insurance Co. in Grand Rapids, Mich. "We need to relate it to the element of risk," he explains. "In banking, for example, in five robberies, the robbers will get only $10,000. But in a case of computer fraud, a single robbery may net 20 times as much."

Survey respondents also say they intend to scale back their plans to purchase minicomputer and mainframe access control software and call-back modems. In 1988, nearly 86% of computer security professionals said they planned to access control products, but about 75% said they planned to purchase those products in 1991, the NCCCD report notes. Some of this decrease is indicative of the shift from mini and mainframe computers to local-area networks.

The media focus on hackers and viruses has led top management to believe that the nation's communications networks are more at risk than a corporation's host computers. Security managers are looking to secure their systems from outside intrusion — not from within, where the greatest risk lies — to alleviate top management concerns.

"No one wants to tell them that the people from the outside are not the true risk," one expert says. "The employees are the greatest threat."

The survey's respondents come from a variety of industries, with banking, military, government, and aerospace representing the greatest concentrations. Retail businesses were surprisingly underrepresented, suggesting a possible lack of computer security consciousness in this portion of the economy, the NCCCD reports.

Top Management Support A Key Factor

Security is frequently considered tedious and the costs of implementing and managing a security program seem greater than the risks, but the consequences of fraud can be crippling. According to experts, over 90 percent of the companies that depend on electronic systems and experience a serious disruption of their data processing operations go out of business. Thus it is easy to understand why selling security to management is one of the most important responsibilities of security professionals.

Automobile makers have learned that air bags, anti-lock brakes and other safety features can help sell automobiles. The idea that safety can be good for business can also be used by security professionals to sell computer security procedures and policies to upper management, according to Charles Wood, a security consultant with Information Integrity of Sausalito, Calif.

Although top managers are becoming increasingly security minded, they have not realized the true potential of information security, Wood says. "Top management's support for information security can be bolstered by showing that superior information security can provide significant competitive advantage," Wood contends.

"Let's no longer discuss the negatives about security but the positives," Wood says. "It's time to shift the conversation to speak about management's concerns such as quality, lower costs, integrity of information and uninterrupted services to customers."

Corporate America relies heavily on its information technology in order to be more competitive and to operate more efficiently. When technology fails, the corporation is at risk, according to Wood. "I suggest that information security be aligned with the strategic goals of the firm."

What are the benefits of investing in information security? According to Wood, there are at least four: improved image of the organization as a conscientious corporate citizen; enhanced customer confidence; new products and services; and new security features for existing products and services.

Companies that are seen as taking a progressive stance on protecting information will win the approval and support of their customers and business partners and the public in general, Wood asserted.

An effective information security effort can be a source of new products and services. First Interstate Bank of California recently suffered a serious fire in one of its large buildings, Wood relates. Fortunately, the bank has a well-tested contingency plan. The bank's ability to quickly recover was widely noted in the press and prompted the bank to go on to offer courses on how to prepare computer contingency plans.

Information security practitioners can justify additional information security efforts on the basis that they would provide another reason for customers to buy an organization's products and services, according to Wood.

"For example, Tandem Computer has been very successful because its systems provide continuous processing even when various failures take place," Wood says.

When promoting the importance and value of information security to top management, security practitioners must "embrace the more aggressive disciples of marketing and sales and shift their focus from unappealing negative conversations to appealing positive conversations," Wood concluded.

Insuring Against Information Theft and Viruses

When the thief who cleaned out a tax consultant's office in Silicon Valley realized that one of the personal computers he had stolen contained client tax records, he downloaded the information from its hard disk onto 20 floppies and mailed them to the victim.

The sympathetic thief realized that without the tax returns, the consultant would quickly be out of business. "It's the only case so far in which the thief recognized that the information had more value than the PC itself," says Donn Parker, a security expert at SRI International, a management consulting firm in Menlo Park, Calif.

It is probably inevitable, Parker warns, that at least some thieves will start realizing that the real money is not in fencing stolen PCs but in reselling the information they contained to a company's competitors or holding it for ransom to its owners.

"Information theft" is being given a careful mulling over by many insurance and security executives these days. How to define and value information so that it can be properly protected, even insured, is much more of an issue, in part because PCs are now so common in corporate America.

The Information Systems Security Association Inc.'s Corresponding Committee on Information Valuation has spent more than a year hammering out definitions that it hopes will enable the insurance industry and others to define and value information.

"Use common-sense procedures to protect the data, not the box."

"Can the potential value of information be insured?" asked Mark Haack, director of marketing, electronics and information technology at St. Paul Fire and Marine Insurance Co. in St. Paul, Minn. "That is the tricky part, and a number of people in the insurance and information industries are trying to come up with an answer for it," he says. "It's an emerging area of risk management that requires more work."

Most insurance companies are going to be skeptical of whatever value a company wants to place on its information, Haack pointed out. If the company recognizes that its information is valuable, then it would be better off looking at ways to minimize the potential of losing it, he says. "Use common-sense procedures to protect the data, not the box."

Even the most rudimentary computer equipment policy will cover the cost of reproducing information lost to theft or other means, but none cover the value of the information itself.

Putting a value on a company's information would be difficult, even if insurance to cover it were available, says Michael Ridgway, vice-president of systems at Grange Insurance Co. in Columbus, Ohio. "Obviously, the cost to re-key the data is infinitesimal compared to the actual value of the data itself in the wrong hands," he says.

It is difficult to put a value on information because it is often intangible, and its value goes beyond whatever it costs to acquire, develop or maintain it.

What use is made of the information, its criticality to the mission of the organization, how long the organization can go without the information and several other factors contribute to the value of information.

Information also has different values to different groups. Authorized users of a company's information may not even recognize that the information has value beyond its identifiable costs, for example, a thief who absconds with the company's secrets to sell them to the highest bider.

Though a firm's insurance policy may not specifically mention computer viruses, there is a good chance that it will cover damages caused by an attack.

"The general conclusion of the insurance industry is that if a corporation's data or even hardware is destroyed or damaged by a virus, they will be covered," says John Lamberson, a software industry specialist at Corroon & Black Corp., an insurance brokerage firm.

Damages caused by a virus fall under the heading of vandalism and malicious mischief, a provision that is common to even the most basic electronic information system insurance policies, Lamberson says.

The recent spate of news reports about viruses has alarmed insurance providers, but after careful reflection, "they have concluded that viruses do not pose an unacceptable risk," Lamberson notes. "Damage from a virus is not unlike the damage that would result from power failures or employee errors."

A handful of insurance companies offer or plan to offer policies specifically aimed at protecting computer users against virus attacks, but Lamberson says he doubts that it will become an industry-wide practice.

"I think we'll see instead a heck of a lot more attention paid by insurance companies to the basic security procedures taken by the insured," Lamberson says.

Chapter 9:

Vulnerability of Corporate Communications Systems

"When the entire contents of the Library of Congress can be stored in a cabinet the size of a briefcase — and transferred from New York to Nairobi in considerably less than one second — there is no denying that we are talking about a fundamentally new world order."

— William T. Esrey, Chairman, United Telecom/US Sprint

They are called "high-tech street gangs" by one law enforcement official, and they use corporate voice-mail computer systems and private branch exchanges to carry out their crimes to the tune of perhaps $5 billion a year, often with impunity.

The victims rarely acknowledge their losses publicly and cooperate in prosecuting the offenders even less often. Law enforcement officials say they can investigate only a fraction of the cases; those that make it to court, they say, often fall victim to unsympathetic judges and juries.

Is it any wonder that telephone "phreaks" — i.e., computer hackers who specialize in ripping off telephone service and other crimes — are "obsessed with data and voice networks?" asks Gail Thackeray, an Arizona law enforcer who has prosecuted several computer crime cases.

The phreaks use voice-mail systems as electronic street corners to exchange such information as stolen credit card numbers and long-distance telephone access codes. They target PBXs—especially those that allow access to international telephone lines—to make telephone calls that are ultimately billed to the PBX owner.

The phreaks are not merely the stereotypical youthful hackers who steal telephone service or break into corporate computer systems for kicks, law enforcement officials say. Frequently, they use PBX and voice-mail systems to facilitate the carrying out of more traditional crimes, according to Jim Black, Coordinator of the Computer-Crime Unit in the Fraud Section of the Los Angeles Police Department (LAPD). The LAPD computer-crime unit is one of only a handful of such units operated by police agencies in the country.

"Looking at the telephone bills of compromised PBX systems, we see that most of the calls are being made to Colombia and other Latin American countries or the Middle East and are related to drug deals," Black says.

> ### "PBX fraud is a closely guarded, dirty little secret held by many companies," says one federal law enforcer

---

In only two months in the summer of 1990, computer hackers rang up $430,000 in unauthorized telephone charges on a private branch exchange (PBX) belonging to Mitsubishi International Corp.

Mitsubishi is suing AT&T in U.S. District Court for allegedly failing to warn it of the risk of fraud and for not responding quickly enough to identify and combat the source of the problem. Mitsubishi filed the suit in response to threats of legal action by AT&T seeking payment for the unauthorized charges.

Who is responsible for picking up the tab when fraud occurs is often a matter of dispute, unless the liability for charges resulting from a security breach is spelled out in a contract, says Brian Moir, legal counsel for the International Communications Association in Washington, D.C. "The carrier, the systems integrator if there was one, the equipment vendor and the customer should know ahead of time the warrants and responsibilities if there is a problem."

Estimates of losses as a result of PBX fraud vary widely, but experts agree that the figure amounts to many millions of dollars per year.

"PBX fraud is a closely guarded, dirty little secret held by many companies," says one federal law enforcer. "The highest figure that I have run into is $1.4 million, lost by one company over a four-day holiday weekend."

Calculating the cost of telephone theft by these high-tech street gangs may be impossible because the victims seldom come forth. "I have heard figures that range between $500 million and $5 billion per year . . . it may be even higher," says a U.S. assistant district attorney for the Northern District of Illinois.

Victims of voice-mail and PBX fraud — both corporate owners of these systems and telecommunications carriers — are seldom willing to prosecute out of fear that the publicity will prompt other phreaks to attack their systems. They also fret that the publicity could be bad for business. One "very large East Coast business lost $1 million in only a few days" but decided to absorb the loss rather than prosecute, according to Black.

"I can pick up the phone any time of the day, call a voice-mail system and get into a box that has been compromised and get stolen credit card numbers, long-distance telephone access numbers and other information, but unless the victim cooperates, I can't investigate," Black says.

Furthermore, some telephone carriers are reluctant to assist in prosecutions out of fear of violating the Electronic Communications Privacy Act (ECPA) of 1986, which prohibits them from monitoring the conversations on their telephone lines.

In a situation that could be taken from the pages of Catch-22, the victim could theoretically be sued for invasion of privacy by the hacker. "Regardless of the individual being attacked or the hacker doing it, they are both our customers, and we have the responsibility of protecting them equally," says Bill Bourke, manager of risk management security at Bell Atlantic.

"The bad guy gets rights, and the telephone company gets sued," a frustrated Thackeray says. "There is no clear statement that says that if the system is under attack, the owner must have [the] right under limited circumstances to eavesdrop in order to protect that system. In the day of the virus and worm, we cannot say anything else."

The long-distance carriers, U.S. Sprint Communications Co. and MCI Communications Corp., in particular, are outstanding examples of cooperation, but the local telephone companies are stubborn as an overly-burdened mule, according to Thackeray.

When phreaks sneak into a company's private branch exchange (PBX) system, they are mainly out to crack the password to an "extender code" that will allow them to route their telephone calls through the PBX onto long-distance telephone lines.

Unlike a telephone credit card holder, the PBX owner is liable for the long-distance calls that the phreaks make using the system.

"Some companies don't suspect that there is a problem until they get a telephone bill that is delivered to them in boxes by UPS instead of in an envelope," says William Cook, a former U.S. assistant district attorney for the Northern District of Illinois.

The billing cycle for PBX systems is typically a month, so the unauthorized use of the system can go on for several days before it is detected. Meanwhile, losses can mount rapidly, often exceeding $10,000 per day.

"The PBX fad is the absolutely worst problem right now because telephone carriers, especially the long-distance carriers, have increased security and their ability to catch people so much that the phreaks are going after PBXs instead," says Thackeray,.

PBX systems are also attractive to phreaks because tracing a telephone call that is routed through a PBX is often difficult and time-consuming.

Voice-mail systems are under attack because they allow phreaks to easily exchange illegally obtained access codes and credit card numbers with impunity because the calls are difficult to trace.

Law enforcement officials complain that companies that use voice-mail systems often install them without an adequate understanding of their security. The systems are too easy to break into because the passwords are easy to decipher or because default passwords have been left intact. Often, the system is administered by a person who does not understand that a voice-mail system is in fact a computer system and should be made as secure as a computer used for accounting and billing.

"They have a brand-new system but don't understand the risks or vulner-abilities," says David Wexler, information systems security manager at Bell Atlantic Corp. "The risks are similar for voice mail, PBX, an operations system for manufac-turing or a mainframe for billing. They are not less secure and can be made as secure as any other computer." He suggests that the voice-mail system administra-tion and security be turned over to IS professionals who are trained in aspects of computer security.

New Communications Technologies Pose Risk

Information technologies that make business faster, easier and more conve-nient than ever before have opened up entirely new vectors of vulnerability for businesses, creating inviting routes of penetration for corporate spies.

Using any information technology, as a matter of course, incurs its own particular risk. The fax, cellular phone, inter-plant microwave link — who could do business without these information vehicles? These days, very few companies.

Who then, can disregard how these technologies of convenience may be tools for the intruder as well as for the user? No one. Never before has doing business been so convenient, yet never before have corporate spies had the opportunities that they have now.

The array of communications media and technologies is multiplying rapidly while location of resources is being decentralized, as distributed computer processing allows users faster access to information resources and greater computing power. The capacity to deliver information and processing power wherever it is needed is the real engine of enterprise in the Information Age.

Many corporate communications networks are poorly designed for security

Larger communication networks create more functionality and more exposures to penetration at the same time. Remember, the value of a data network is increased in direct proportion to the number of locations it can access. The trouble is exposure to infiltration is increased in direct proportion to the number of connections a communications device makes.

That means an infiltrator who has found an entrance at one point in the network may very well be able to roam over the entire network. A private business exchange (PBX) that handles 90 percent of all call traffic in a company offers its owners centralized, easy to manage, communications hardware. A tapper who gets into that PBX, though, has access to the same percentage of the company's telephone traffic.

In the same way, if your computer network allows users free range over the system and easy access to any and all files, a mercenary hacker who penetrates that network will have the same ease of access.

Look at the exposure to risk in the communications technologies at hand in any American company: Centrex phone service offered by local Bell Operating Companies, the PBX dedicated business phone exchange, the satellite downlink, microwave transmission, cellular telephones and the corporate spy's favorite target, the fax machine.

Companies simply cannot operate without the convenience, speed and benefits that these technologies offer. Neither can they continue to operate them without consideration of the ways they can be exploited by unscrupulous competitors.

With the world at peace and new competitors emerging from every corner of the globe, the American corporation that succeeds must be lean, innovative and, most importantly if any of its efforts are to succeed, information secure.

Many corporate communications networks are poorly designed for security. The primary criteria for selecting networks too often speaks to finding the lowest cost solution. The guiding principles of network design, however, are wide connectivity, universal access for company personnel and ease of maintenance for network managers. Companies will pay money for "those" features but security is most often considered a separate issue, something to be considered after purchasing systems and service contracts.

Future Trends in Corporate Communications

The demand for corporate telecommunications services is rapidly increasing with companies offering electronic data interchange, information storage, and E-mail. Companies very often are outsourcing their entire telecommunications operation to a third party company that will provide hardware, maintenance and staffing. In virtually none of the cases is security and increased vulnerability of these services considered.

Many existing systems have older technology which do not have security features, strong access control or audit trails. They were designed with performance, not security, in mind. Even today, security considerations must wrestle with the perennial objection that security routines inhibit access by users.

Companies with a mobile sales or maintenance force or a large contingent of outside contractors also must have a system open enough for their employees to use no matter where they are, including in their homes and on the road.

The portable office is a new concept with high security vulnerability because it involves remote access and radio links. The office can now span the globe, be extended into any den, kitchen or hotel room in the world, places that do not have the same information security level as the office.

Some people now utilize portable PCs from their hotel rooms or even hook PCs and faxes up to cellular radios, easy targets for eavesdropping. Every keystroke, including passwords and access codes that are transmitted over a system is available to anyone who wishes to intercept that communication.

Interception is possible with high quality, off-the-shelf hardware that 10 years ago existed only in the professional intelligence services of the world, but now is available to anyone, including competitors, hackers and free-lance information thieves. Combatting these privateers is less a work of inspiration in the heat of battle and more a thoughtful preparation for long-term siege.

To that end, for information to be secure, companies must eschew bean-counting methods when selecting communications equipment and services and, instead, factor in the potential losses they could expect if their competitors were able to intercept their day-to-day communications.

Executives and security managers should consider the value of the information and the vulnerability of the media their companies use. These considerations are important qualities in determining design criteria for a communications network.

The telephone cannot be taken for granted. How user-friendly a company's phone system will be to its owner — and how hostile it will be to intruders — depends on the decisions the company makes when it assembles its communications network.

The trend in telecommunications requirements are: faster and lower cost long-haul service and access to more (and bigger) databases by more people in scattered geographic locations. For reasons of perception, though, usually it is the computer systems that get the benefit of a security envelope. When companies contract for private telecommunication networks, invariably, keeping costs low is a major factor and little or no thought is given to the protection of the information against corporate wiretappers.

This practice flies in the face of technical realities and recent history. The first international computer privateers were by necessity "phone freaks" versed in the mechanics of stealing long distance service by breaking the phone company's central office codes. As deregulation takes information on communications technologies further from the hands of the AT&T priesthood, the distribution of knowledge on how to crack phone systems can only increase.

Corporate networks offer tappers faster returns than public switched networks; they are far easier to wiretap for voice communications or rig for computer data interception. It is primarily dedicated to the function of the corporation, which means information on the network is not mixed in with non-corporate information. This allows a single penetration to accrue maximum data interception.

This centralization also reduces the amount of work an infiltrator must perform to tap into the right phone lines. Instead of, say, hiring a proxy to sift through lines at a Bell Company's central offices, calling back and trying to fool the company's employees into confirming the phone numbers of the lines they are tapping, a tapper who manages to break into a PBX has already done all the searching he needs.

Centrex service, which is marketed by local Bell operating companies is a much more vulnerable system than an on-site PBX. With Centrex service, all calls go "downtown" to a Bell operating company's central office, even calls from one desk to another on the same floor. Therefore, either a wiretapper on the path between the company and the central office or a compromised person within the central office has access to all the information the company moves through its Centrex service.

In truth, anyone with access to that central office can hear what is going through the company and — given the off-site maintenance features of modern central offices — a smart, mercenary hacker can have as much access as phone company repair personnel. Remember, the central office is another computer, something that can be penetrated and marshalled for use by competitors.

Phone company personnel are as corruptible as any and, during this era of deregulation when contract negotiations are taking on a bitter edge, phone company employees may be even more willing to tap a line for a certain consideration. Though convictions for wiretapping is rare, the cases that do appear in court, indicate that tapping is rampant and almost impossible to detect. One case in Ohio suggests how prevalent wiretapping by phone company personnel may be.

Cincinnati Bell employee Leonard Gates was fired for tapping lines at the Bell Company's central offices in 1986 but when he went to court over the matter, Gates testified in 1988 that his superiors ordered him to place about 1,200 taps on phone lines without appropriate law enforcement warrants. Gates allegedly tapped the phones of three members of Congress, federal judges, local politicians, lawyers and businesses. One of the alleged targets was a General Electric jet-engine plant that Gates balked at tapping since he feared the plant's defense contracts could put him in line for an espionage charge if he were caught.

PBXs, while preferable to Centrex service for most applications in terms of its inaccessibility to adversaries, have their vulnerabilities and offer, of course, the sweetened attraction of concentrating company communications through a single point, simplifying surreptitious monitoring. Most have the capacity for remote maintenance — like central offices — though dial-up. Compromise of the maintenance password can result in massive service fraud and data loss. To illustrate their vulnerability is the fact that PBX fraud by outside dialing and penetration is a growing problem.

Calculating the Costs and Benefits of Communications

Just as companies weigh the costs and benefits of the features that their phone systems offer, so must they also weigh the cost and benefits of those technologies in terms of their hardness against security breaches. The media that carries corporate communications is important in securing the company's information. Consider these communications technologies and their vulnerabilities:

- Satellite is clearly the most vulnerable media because of its broad downlink footprint which more or less broadcasts the transmissions over a large area. Such a downlink could bring corporate information raining down onto the dish antennas of competitors.

- Long-distance microwave transmission is the next most vulnerable.

- Cellular telephone is very vulnerable over a short range because of its omnidirectional transmission coverage. (Who can forget the brouhaha a few years back over gubernatorial candidate Charles Robb whose campaign supporters intercepted some of Virginia Governor Douglas Wilder's cellular phone calls.)

- Point-to-point microwave is relatively directional, but is dedicated to a specific facility, more difficult to intercept but easier to sift through.

- Land line, hard wire, coaxial and fiber — in that order — are the least vulnerable.

Managers whose businesses are shopping for phone systems would do well to guard against the bean-counting myopia that produces short-term gains on the spread sheet. That gain could return a pat on the back, maybe a bonus, but the long term losses to the company that has had its telecommunications system compromised could undermine the entire business.

Technologies of Convenience: A Double-Edged Sword

Technologies of convenience like the cellular telephone, third party electronic mail and the facsimile machine are accepted by American corporations with all the enthusiasm of kids with new toys. These toys have some sharp edges that have to be considered before they are integrated into the corporate communications environment.

Cellular is wide open to interception. Soon after cellular nets were installed in U.S. cities and the squiggly little antennas were mounted on cars, stories about embarrassing intercepts hit a lot of local papers. The openness of the media was for some users, never even considered. The best rule of thumb for using cellular phones is to assume that all calls are being overheard unless an encryption device is used.

Electronic mail systems are run, in some cases, by commercial services with little or no security. The operators of these services have little incentive to install security checks, primarily because customers do not demand it. Who'd want to frustrate fickle customers with more ID authentication checks? It is also impossible to detect a surreptitious reading of mail by a system operator unless the sender encrypts it before transmission.

If the corporate spy would name one darling of his trade it would have to be the modern, full-featured fax. It's convenient; one has to monitor the line; and once it is tapped, the information thief need only turn on his fax. When the target's fax transmission is activated, the thief's fax will dutifully turn out its own copy of the materials being sent or received. Though that is not the extent of the fax's vulnerability to espionage.

The British press recently detailed electronic spying being carried out from vehicles parked outside buildings with equipment that could read and translate the magnetic field around fax machines.

Faxes with internal memory to store documents can also be robbed easily. Many fax machines with this feature come from the factory with pre-programmed passcode numbers for the stored files. Many businesses simply leave the widely-known factory settings in place. A "faxpionage" agent simply dials in, punches the factory-installed passcode and is rewarded because no one in the company took a moment to reprogram the passcode numbers.

Threats to information security will always be with us. The dynamic that will increase the potential harm by theft and vandalism will be the ever increasing size of corporate databases. In the Information Age, the vaults can only get bigger and richer. The magic of having information available to us everywhere at all times is too powerful to turn away from at this time.

Chapter 10:

Communications Security Methods to Safeguard Proprietary Information

"U.S. executives are unbelievably naive about theft of information assets and electronic eavesdropping. Car phones, phoning and faxing from hotels, and the 'portable office' are all windows for competitors, adversaries and governments to peer into the heart of vital corporate operations."

—— Noel D. Matchett, President, Information Security, Inc.

There was an American electronic company in Asia that was loosing bid after bid after bid for reasons the company's management couldn't fathom. They'd been successful before, so the string of failed bids was especially unsettling. The competition hadn't changed radically, indicating something was wrong in some vector of the enterprise outside of manufacturing and marketing.

The corporate leadership decided to try beefing up information security measures; when they examined their communications network they found a weak link: a microwave connection between company office buildings.

The company encrypted the microwave link and went back to work. Suddenly, their rate of successful bids soared and the cause of that string of failures became evident. Who knows how many of their competitors were listening?

That story, told by information security expert Noel Matchett, president of Information Security, Inc., in Silver Spring, Maryland, is offered as a parable of how critical just one point of leakage can be for the fortunes of a company. The lesson is clear: one application of information security technology saved the company from being driven out of business; that technology should have been in place when the communications network was built.

Truly, given the counter-intelligence technologies available on the market today, there is no excuse for any company's communications networks to go naked into the briars of modern industry, exposed to the thorns of corporate espionage and its refined, chastened sister: corporate intelligence.

COMSEC: Constructive Communications Security

Denying the growing threats against communications security — COMSEC in the vernacular — won't make it go away. Better to engage it constructively with appropriate technologies than to loose business to the competition.

Technologies of infiltration and surreptitious surveillance — such as bugs, telephone tapping devices and tiny transmitters — are becoming better and cheaper all the time, creating a whole new dimension to concepts of physical security. No longer is keeping the adversary out of the plant enough. Now the secure corporation must find and incapacitate its electronic and mechanical proxies.

Corporations with investments in sophisticated computing platforms can appreciate that technology's indispensability in many corporate functions; they can also appreciate how quickly computers become obsolete and require updating, modification and replacement.

Yet companies are content to leave their communications networks virtually unprotected, despite the fact that they have long been made vulnerable by the technologies of information interception. If a company is to stay in business, it must recognize that communications security is as vital a part of its competitive posture as the computing environment. In the Information Age, it's vital to scrutinize the security of the locks on the filing cabinets and consider the thinness of electronic walls believed to offer protection.

Cost effective protection involves taking a total systems approach rather than trying to integrate COMSEC protection piecemeal in an existing system. Security, like quality, is built in at the beginning and is maintained. That means a company must be able to understand its existing security exposures. It requires an understanding of the limits of COMSEC hardening to deal with the security exposures inherent in an existing system.

For a lot of companies, integrating COMSEC technologies will be a reactive process, applying appropriate preventive procedures and hardware to an existing system. That, as a matter of course, can be a troublesome enterprise since the cost of designing COMSEC functionality into a network is totally dependent on how early in the development of that network COMSEC measures are applied. That isn't to say that early designing will guarantee COMSEC measures will be simple and easy to achieve.

Even a relatively limited application presents significant design problems like cable television which is a relatively simple system. Cable TV systems send programming from one point of origin out on coaxial cable to receiving sets in homes, presenting not even half the functional complexity of a full-blown corporate communications system.

Vilified for robbing consumers, cable TV is probably the most heavily pirated subscriber media service in the world. The current technology for protecting satellite and pay TV has been subjected to extensive analysis and has been successfully exploited by video pirates to get free programming they'd normally have to pay to view.

Publicly available documents describe detailed procedures to extract sensitive information from the cable receiving/decoding devices' microprocessors using techniques such as thermal shock, x-rays, and microwave, and provide specific instructions for re-programming the processors and bypassing security checks. This kind of sophistication was brought to bear on a technology for the purpose of getting a free peek at a boxing match or a pornographic film. Imagine the comparative motivation of corporate espionage agents employed in the active interception of trade secrets.

Compared to complex corporate communications systems, cable television networks are relatively simple to secure, indicating the level of protection companies really need to provide to be truly information secure. The trouble is, as corporate networks are coupled and systems integrated, protection is almost always an afterthought — if considered at all.

The more complex and far flung the interconnections of the network are, the tougher it is to secure the network after the fact. This dynamic determines how cost-effective —or how doable — refitting a communications network for COMSEC will be.

COMSEC Planning and Implementation

Creating a system from scratch, security costs could run from two percent to five percent of total system costs. Refitting an existing system, pieced together over time from a variety of hardware and networks, could cost 20% or more of the system cost. At a certain point of expansion and complexity, it becomes cheaper to simply start from scratch and design COMSEC into a new system than trying to retrofit a network to achieve an acceptable level of security.

Companies should understand which security systems protect information that, if lost, could jeopardize the survival of the company. The key to appropriate systems design is understanding what the adversary's capabilities are, as well as the range of technical attacks and approaches that can be used to crack a security system. Knowing one's own weaknesses as well as a potential adversary's strengths is key to planning for security.

The techniques of COMSEC have been proven time and time again, so there's every reason to proceed with the objective of achieving an acceptable level of security for the total system.

Oil companies and toy companies have been practitioners of total communications systems security for many years because of the high cost lax information security can be to their particular enterprises.

Oil companies have encrypted their vital information transmissions for over 50 years. When an exploration company hits a wildcat well, it doesn't want others to know and thereby have a first crack at the leases. For much the same reason, oil companies try to be very quiet about where any new drilling takes place.

The dynamics of toy manufacturing have forced toy companies to create large, highly trained intelligence and security forces. Since it is very easy for a rival to quickly copy and market a toy one competitor's company is launching, security is vital. Just one hint of what a company's featured holiday offerings will be can cost that company millions.

Some toy companies boast of world-wide alarm systems that are operated from central consoles that cover the company's facilities all over the globe. Analyst Matchett says toy companies' security forces can be every bit as good as a Top Secret government intelligence agency.

Communications security technologies are available in as many different price ranges and choices as there are for, say, electronic testing equipment. In larger corporations, because of the complexity of today's information networks and the growing multitude of protection options, employing a skilled security architect is virtually a necessity for an effective solution at lowest cost. Containing costs is always easier for someone who knows the market, knows the problem, and can pick the appropriate, lowest cost solutions.

Cost of COMSEC Coming Down

The good news is even the most advanced protection is rapidly coming down in price. Currently, government agencies and U.S. defense contractors are using a secure communications telephone handset called the STU-III which can encrypt voice or data communications.

The STU-III was developed by NSA and is selling for around $2000 — a considerable discount from the STU-II it replaced. A program to make the instrument available on the commercial market is underway. A growing array of commercial products are available that provide secure telephonic communications, presumably less effective than the STU-III but powerful nonetheless.

Cryptography of computer data is also being revolutionized by so-called public key cryptographic systems — considered the strongest yet by many industry analysts. In public key cryptographic systems, the user publishes his "public key" and correspondents use it to encrypt messages to the user. The only key that can decrypt the message is the user's "secret key."

In this way, the public key method provides encryption and authentication of the receiver's identity. From a security standpoint, if correctly implemented, a significant improvement in security is provided. Like any system, however, the specific applications and implementation are extremely important.

The U.S. government has yet to certify public key encryption systems for non-government use; the politics of that omission are too complex to plumb here, but it is fair to say lack of government standards on public key cryptography does create some difficulty in product selection. Except for those allowed to purchase government endorsed systems, there is no guarantee of an effectively implemented key management system.

Security assessment, design and implementation is not the role for an amateur and requires a comprehensive set of skills to develop and implement solutions. On the other hand, senior management is the catalyst and must be sensitive to the broad general issues and the potential impact upon corporate survival from loss of information via inadequately protected systems. Senior management has got to realize the need for COMSEC measures if the firm expects to remain competitive.

Security Components of COMSEC Model

Communications security has traditionally been defined as the amalgamation of three elements: physical security, emission security and cryptographic security, conceptually separate, though in practice three mutually dependent elements of COMSEC. Even examining COMSEC from the most evident vector, physical security, it quickly becomes apparent that all the elements of the communications system must be considered simultaneously. The complexity of the modern communications network demands all elements be totally secure if the network in total is to be secure.

By physical security, we mean the protection of sensitive facilities and technical information that could compromise the security of the communications network. Access control devices are becoming more and more vital to the secure operation of a system since computers can't differentiate from a legitimate user and an impostor, especially one that has commandeered an unattended terminal that a registered user has logged onto for full privileges.

Even such obvious elements as subverting a microcomputer-based alarm system installed to protect sensitive information must be considered. In Europe, most alarm systems and protective services are encrypted. In the United States encrypted alarm systems — where users must possess a cryptographic key to arm and disarm the system — are rarities. Unencrypted alarm systems are even certified by the Department of Defense.

Physical security means more than just keeping the spies out of the building. It also includes preventing intruders from stealing cryptographic keys from out of a safe or from an off-site user. Physical security also refers to such routines, as enforcing policies relating to encrypting and decrypting communications and destroying keying material when it is no longer needed.

Emission security refers to the containment of information born by signals radiating into the air or coupling to other paths outside of the secure environment, such as power lines. Some technologies, like the microwave facilities of the American electronics company at the beginning of this chapter may be obvious exposures. Others, like the London "faxpionage" case, are not so apparent — until, of course, the intruders are caught and appear on the front page of the local newspapers.

Corporations must match the degree of protection with the progressive technological capacity of their adversaries

---

Traditionally, emissions security has been reserved for the classified government market. What corporation would ever imagine it would have to combat the kinds of emission security situations like, say, the publicized problems the U.S. State Department had to face in debugging the Moscow embassy?

Unfortunately, in today's climate most American businesses in the international marketplace are faced with exactly that. In most cases, however, esoteric emission attacks need not be addressed since the threats are far more obvious and more basic security work needs to be accomplished before advanced protection techniques are needed.

For sensitive information believed to be pursued by adversaries, there are emissions control technologies developed under the National Security Agency's TEMPEST program, expensive, though totally effective in combatting emissions leakage. TEMPEST technologies most often involve shielding hardware with materials to block radio transmissions built into hardware and the rooms where the hardware is kept.

Cryptography is the science of scrambling information, usually text or spreadsheets in the corporate environment, using a mathematical construct — an algorithm — that translates readable text into a form that would be impossible to read without the algorithmic process and the variable it is combined with to vary the encryption.

Without the algorithm and variable, a so-called key to filter the information, it is impossible to translate it back into readable form. It can function as a piece of hardware that can read cards containing keys but these days most all cryptographic engines are combinations of hardware, firmware, and software written especially for that application.

Who hasn't spent an evening watching a late night movie on television about the determined efforts of allied code breakers to crack the encryption keys of Axis armies? The war is still on, but happily, algorithms are available to industry today that are believed to be uncrackable with current technology, most notably the Data Encryption Standard (DES) that is certified by NSA.

For over 10 years the DES algorithm has withstood an extremely aggressive analysis in the public domain from both academic and corporate mathematicians. Result: no reliable method of cracking DES has been found to date. However, no algorithm is secure forever, if for no other reason than the advance of technology which ultimately may allow an opponent to test all possible key settings in a reasonable time. Like all technologies, corporations must match the degree of protection with the progressive technological capacity of their adversaries.

Cryptographic security today also involves the security of the algorithm itself and the key distribution system — which also frequently involves its own cryptographic protections system. In older systems, the key was a setting printed on a piece of paper or a punched card that was used to set up the machine. The entire security of the system depended on protecting the key, from creation, through distribution and use, until final destruction.

A much more comprehensive analysis of the cryptographic system design is necessary to ensure the security of today's complex systems, which in many cases are integrated into the telecommunications components. Therefore, an exploitable security weakness in the key distribution system can lead to compromise of the entire network.

Results of just one breach of the security of the key distribution system can be devastating. The Walker-Whitworth spy case in 1986 is illustrative of the power inherent in having possession of a target's keys.

The U.S. government testified publicly that one million classified messages were read by the KGB because Mr. Whitworth delivered cryptographic keys, enabling the Soviets to decrypt U.S. military traffic. It was even reported that this one man's actions could have tipped the scales of a conflict between the U.S. and the Soviets in favor of the Soviet Union should a war have broken out. Such was the value of the information that should have been protected but was not.

The Vulnerabilities of Humanware

This same case also illustrates the damage that just one disloyal employee can visit upon his employer. In COMSEC, a great deal of the dialogue revolves around the exposure of communications technologies. Humanware should never be overlooked, however, or taken for granted. A survey last year by an industrial security association, in fact, points to employees as the most prodigious vessels for secret information leaking out of corporations.

The lesson is clear: know your employees. First and foremost, check out an applicant's every reference and if there are chronological holes in their resumes, make them explain them to your satisfaction. Assume an applicant could be a "mole" in the employ of a competitor. Confirm the past relationships of all existing employees. Even the most credible of employees must be reexamined since the best moles are solid employees with a record of achievement, with access and the trust of company executives.

Consider the costs in morale a big layoff can mean on the shop floor — or even a promotion of one peer worker over another. Employees seeing families of former co-workers struggling can harbor ill-will and plot mayhem or treachery to avenge themselves and friends against the company.

Those employees who know the company's business are the single greatest potential source of information for competitors

---

Matchett's files are full of disgruntled employee stories. There was one case a few years ago on the west coast of an electronic manufacturer who was loosing lots of bids — suspiciously by only a very slim percentage over a period of two and a half years.

The company's security personnel put in an extra computer audit trail and caught a disgruntled employee who had access to bids and pricing information. He could see the computer files from the people who drafted proposals, and he was passing it off to competitors. Why would he vandalize his own company for no profit? Revenge. The employee had been passed over for promotion in favor of another coworker.

In another extreme instance a Pacific Telesis worker, enraged, pumped over 200 shotgun shells into a central office, disrupting service and completely destroying the switch.

Bottom-line thinking has its place, but the costs of driving a work force toward militancy is always more than can be predicted. Those employees who know the company's business are the single greatest potential source of information for competitors. Giving them reasons to stay loyal is only in the company's best interest.

All the hardware and cryptography in the world, however, no matter how elegantly assembled, will not ensure a totally secure environment without the intelligent participation of personnel and integration of security regimes into the workaday cadence of the office or manufacturing environment.

A combination of administrative regulations and technical testing must be put in place to maintain a current and relatively "clean" network, i.e. one with a minimum of unregistered or unauthorized and unprotected connections. Frequently, employees connect unhardened access ports to the network with dial-in modems, creating exposures that should be closed.

Computer access audit reports that record users activities should be examined scrupulously. If they are untenably large, the programming that generates them should be modified to filter out of the report all but truly suspicious events. Those events should be investigated. Remember, the Hanover Hackers were pursued and finally caught by a University of California at Berkeley computer systems operator who discovered a 75-cent discrepancy between the connect time of authorized users and the amount of charged usage time that the computer recorded.

Tracking down anomalies to their sources and eliminating the unauthorized accesses regularly tempers the communications system and keeps it hardened against intruders in the way that mending a dike ensures a tighter seal against sea water leakage.

Employees, and users of the corporate communications system, must be made to understand the investment they have in the security of the network, how it could affect the future of the company and even the security of their own jobs.

As well, observation identity authentication routines will become important for users as a means of protecting their reputations when companies begin accounting for users' time on the system, according to Natick, Mass-based security analyst Sanford Sherizen. No one would want to be wrongly accused of improper use of computing resources, given the notoriety it could bring.

Corporate Spy Tools of the Trade

The future of corporate espionage is already here. Once the tools of the government law enforcement agencies and the intelligence community, these technologies are available in a variety never imagined 20 years ago.

The technologies of communications attack make up a daunting ordnance which proves that war has been declared. Finding equipment for espionage applications is as easy as using the phone book. Look under surveillance to find a local supplier. Finding them is no more difficult than locating a hardware store or stereo shop.

Bugs, telephone taps that will pick up every sound in the room and miniaturized cameras are all for sale, or for rent if you want to save the costs of capitalizing all that equipment.

Magazines for radio hobbyists flaunt advertisements for bugs and eavesdropping equipment and even computer programs that allow a computer to monitor multiple channels on just about any usable frequency band.

One catalog by a U.S. company, Surveillance Technology Group in Port Chester, N.Y. lists eight areas in which it produces equipment with the following functions: photo/video surveillance; telecommunications intercepts; sound intercepts; alternative sound intercepts (infrared, laser, ultra sounds, fiber optics); radio intercept; locating and tracking; tactical alarm systems; covert communications.

Fortunately, the technologies of counter-espionage have kept apace with the growth of information interception hardware. One retail concern, a company called Communications Control System (CCS) that has sales offices in the U.S., Europe and the Middle East, publishes lists of counter-spy equipment every bit as good as the offerings for spying equipment in the trade magazines.

In one CCS product list, the company proffers wiretap detectors, telephone scramblers, tape recorder detectors, bomb detectors, bullet-proof vehicles and apparel, kidnap tracing systems and infrared viewers. In another listing, the company adds lie detectors and miniature pocket-sized bug detectors.

At any one time CCS provides materials and services to three-fourths of the Fortune 500. That echelon of achievement is hard won. Most of the Fortune 500 have decided that counter-espionage technologies are extremely important if they are to maintain there competitive position in the marketplace.

Today, as never before, to become a Fortune 500 company will mean being information-tight and ready for the prying, spying and attempted infiltrations of competitors. As the traditions of European war-fighting were discarded during the American Revolution, so has the principles of gentlemanly business in the Information Age.

Corporations that once sought merely profit, now seek market dominance; companies that eschewed the black magic of corporate espionage embrace it. The era when the honor of men was thought enough to ensure that capitalist enterprise followed certain written and unwritten rules, has waned.

Chapter 11:

How the U.S. Government Protects Critical Information

"Despite global events of the past year and the easing of East-West tensions, the United States still has secrets that must be protected — secrets that would be beneficial to foreign powers — secrets that, if lost, would be detrimental to our national interests."

— *John F. Donnelly, Director, Defense Investigative Service*

T he American government protects critical information of national importance through a large but hidden bureaucracy, employing exotic technology and simple hard work under the authority of a complex set of rules and statutes. American business can learn much from what government does. While their goals may differ, as well as the constraints on what each may do, the basic task is the same: to get sensitive information to people who need it and to keep it from everyone else.

Several examples of cooperation between business and government to safeguard secrets already exist. The biggest is the Pentagon's Defense Industrial Security Program (DISP), set up to protect military information entrusted to U.S. industry. Over 10,000 private defense contractors and nearly two million of their employees are authorized to handle defense secrets. Altogether, they possess more than 14 million classified documents.

DISP and related programs, however, are concerned only with defense-related secrets, information of direct concern to the government. Thwarting industrial espionage of other types is the responsibility of private companies themselves, with the FBI and state agencies becoming involved only if laws are broken.

The private sector has not thrown the same proportion of resources at problems of security as has the federal government. DISP and other such programs grew out of the experiences of World War II and the Cold War, driven by fears about the defense of the nation. Yet a private company's survival may depend just as much as the nation's on safeguarding its information.

Some government officials see trends that will make the federal experience in information security even more relevant to the private sector in the years to come. The private sector is now catching up to the public sector in the use of exotic computer and communication technologies, which make information more precarious. Computers have become depositories of sensitive data, phone lines and radio links the channels over which it gets transmitted. A spy no longer must invade a company's or an agency's premises to steal its secrets.

At the same time, the business environment has become more competitive. Competition has become more international, and nations are increasingly turning to economic espionage to gain advantages. The government's experience fighting foreign spies will be needed in the business arena as well.

Business and Government Dissimilar, Alike

In some ways, the case of business is quite different from that of government. There is no concept in the private sphere exactly comparable to national security. Although the market is sometimes figuratively like a battlefield, the bottom line for a company, unlike a government, is profit. A company protects its proprietary information primarily to protect, even to enhance, its profitability. Trade secrets in the hands of a rival or the public at large can cost a company its competitive edge.

Another difference is in the purposes of secrecy. Federal agencies are barred by presidential decree from using secrecy merely to protect themselves or their employees from embarrassing disclosures. The order also bars federal employees from exploiting government classification to shield violations of law, to hide inefficiency, administrative error, or to restrain competition.

By contrast, the public's right to know is absent in the business world. The power of American companies to create secrets is limited only by what the law prevents them from doing, as well as by what the corporate culture judges to be acceptable.

Despite these differences, both government and business are alike in other respects. Both require secrecy. In some ways, their survival can depend on it. Corporations and federal agencies must often protect information to guarantee the rights of employees and contractors. Confidentiality, privacy and due process can be jeopardized by unauthorized disclosures. Finally, the methodology for maintaining secrecy in the public and private sectors is the same.

The government's secrecy system can serve as a model for business. The foundation of the government system has three main parts.

First, there are categories or levels of classification. They are assigned to pieces of information to indicate the degree of damage to national security which could result from unauthorized disclosure or the circle of personnel who are allowed access to it.

Second, there is a process for assigning clearances, which allow individuals determined to be trustworthy access to information of a certain category. Sometimes individuals given clearances are also required to sign secrecy agreements, acknowledging a set of rules on what they can and cannot do with what they learn.

Third, there are methods of document control and physical security to limit physical access to classified information to only those individuals cleared to have it.

These classification categories, clearance procedures and physical-access restrictions control one's access not only to written documents but also to computerized texts, oral briefings and scientific hardware.

Additionally, the system includes public affairs offices, to supervise contacts between people with clearances and people who lack them. There are also "operations security," (OPSEC) units, to identify and eliminate unclassified indicators which uncleared individuals could piece together to infer classified facts. Finally, counterintelligence agents try to identify unauthorized efforts to obtain classified information and eliminate them or at least render them ineffective.

Here is where industry can learn from the experience of the public sector. A program of classification, clearances, and physical security modeled on federal efforts will demonstrate seriousness in protecting secrets. Secrecy oaths also play an important role, since businesses are not restricted by the same First Amendment concerns that limit the government. Companies likewise have needs in the areas of public affairs, operations security and counterintelligence, and they are often very similar to government's.

Private-sector efforts to protect critical information may actually make greater use of the legal system than do federal efforts. Many states make it a crime to steal trade secrets, and even where it is not a crime, victims can more easily sue to enjoin or punish thieves than can the government. To get a court's support, however, a company must show that it has taken reasonable measures to protect its trade secrets.

The Federal Bureaucracy

Thousands of employees scattered throughout the federal government are assigned the task of protecting critical information. Although the Pentagon's security program is the largest and most complex, smaller but similar efforts run throughout the rest of the national security bureaucracy. Whether separately or by sharing resources between agencies, each carries out the basic functions of clearing employees, classifying and declassifying information, and maintaining physical security, and sometimes further responsibilities in counterintelligence, public relations and operations security.

The White House, the Central Intelligence Agency, the Departments of State, Treasury, Justice, Energy, Commerce and Transportation, the Nuclear Regulatory Commission, NASA, the Federal Emergency Management Agency—even the President's personal representative for Micronesian Status Negotiations, during the Carter Administration—have been granted the authority to classify information. These agencies and others grant clearances and physically protect national security information.

Several agencies handle security matters for the federal government as a whole. The Federal Bureau of Investigation, which has its own internal information protection program, also handles government-wide counterintelligence, although FBI officials have in the past been reluctant to launch inquiries in some areas. For example, investigations into the sources of leaks, by which the news media frequently obtain information on an unauthorized basis, have troubled these officials, especially when there has been little chance of prosecution.

A collection of offices at the Commerce, State and Defense Departments oversee export controls; they place sensitive technologies on export-control lists, determine those countries to which sensitive technologies can be exported, and uncover violations. An Information Security Oversight Office oversees classification activities across federal agencies. An interagency committee on information security also exists.

Just how do these agencies protect critical information, and what can the private sector learn from them? Consider classification.

Ideas about public access to government information are different in the United States from what they are in many other countries. Some governments work in inherent secrecy. Protecting government information requires no justification, because it is the nature of government work to be secret. Citizen access to information is not a right but a privilege, awarded only for some specific purpose or after some special act of generosity by some government official.

In the United States, the burden lies with the government to be ready with explanations whenever information is withheld. Only a narrow range of explanations is allowed. The main justification for protecting government information is that release of it to unauthorized persons would cause identifiable damage to national security. Information of this kind ordinarily concerns military weapons or operations, diplomatic activities, espionage or covert action, the handling of nuclear materials, or certain scientific or economic matters of international importance.

Several principles govern classification. The three lowest levels of classification to which a given item of information can be assigned are proportional, roughly, to the degree of damage to national security which could reasonably be expected to result from unauthorized disclosure of the information; these levels are designated Confidential, Secret and Top Secret, and the expected damage, by definition, runs from some, to serious, to exceptionally grave.

Authority to assign these categories emanates, for the most part, from the heads of agencies. In practice, however, the actual business of classifying information is often assisted by standards set out in what are known as security classification guidance documents. This guidance reflects even more general conventions about what ought to be classified.

The DoD, for example, considers questions like the following:

❑   Could unauthorized disclosure of a piece of data benefit another government by reducing the U.S. lead in the development of some weapon system?

❑   Could it enhance foreign military R&D to the detriment of U.S. interests?

❑   Could it improve foreign intelligence and counterintelligence programs?

Some information is classified at even higher levels than Top Secret with designations that are themselves classified. These higher classifications require special handling of information beyond the system by which information at Top Secret and lower are handled.

One form is known as Sensitive Compartmented Information, or SCI. Such information relates to systems used for collecting intelligence, like those at the Central Intelligence Agency and the National Security Agency. The special handling is required in order to protect the sources and methods used in the collection process, since exposure of information obtained by those sources and methods could compromise them and render them vulnerable to countermeasures.

Other forms of higher classification are set up in connection with Special Access Programs. These are created *ad hoc* to handle particularly sensitive information for which normal protection procedures are considered inadequate. So-called "black programs" like the development of the Stealth bomber, carried out behind a veil of not just secrecy but deception, require Special Access Programs.

Classification at all levels is subject to restrictions. It cannot be used to conceal violations of law or unflattering facts. Officials are required to "downgrade" classified information, or to lower its level of classification, according to procedures established when the material is first classified. On documents, this requires a marking which indicates a schedule of downgrading. This same process sets a date for declassifying the information entirely.

Private companies should consider following the example of the government in classifying documents. Doing so could potentially be key to convincing a court of sincerity and dedication in protecting trade secrets in the event of a security breach and may help prevent such problems in the first place.

Corporate secrets consist of proprietary technical data and confidential business information. Such secrets can be appraised in a similar way to those of government by determining which items could benefit competitors and cause potential harm to the company if they became known to others.

Security consultants suggest that documents judged to contain secrets should be labeled as such. They also suggest that documents regularly be declassified, since a company's laxness in this respect could leave courts unimpressed about its claims of confidentiality and of violations thereof: if everything is classified, nothing is special.

Clearances and Secrecy Agreements

Federal employees, contractors and others who need access to classified information are cleared for such access through a process of background investigation. This investigation is directly proportional to the level of classified information they need to accomplish their tasks.

For example, applicants for a Top Secret clearance must complete a lengthy questionnaire which furnishes personal information relative to: family and associates, residences, education, employment history, character references, medical and financial condition, prior arrests, affiliation with organizations, etc. The form requires information covering the 10 years prior to application.

The investigation is conducted by a special agent of the government and consists of a process of verification and information gathering through federal, state and municipal records checks; personal interviews with the applicant, former employers, associates, teachers and neighbors; and a credit history check.

Beginning in 1992 the government instituted the Single-Scope background investigation procedure which has reduced delays in granting clearances. Until recently, applicants had to go through a separate application process for each agency with which they worked, and each agency ran its own separate investigation. During this time, it sometimes became difficult for some officials to gain access to all the information they needed to do their jobs. The new procedure has reduced these problems by making clearances transferable among federal agencies.

Employees in some sensitive positions are required to sign secrecy agreements as a condition of employment. These contracts pledge the signer not to make public classified information learned during his or her employment. Although they are not specific about the consequences in case of a breach, these contracts have been interpreted by the courts to obligate the signer to pre-publication government censorship of his or her writings and confiscation of any profits received in the absence of such censorship.

This is as far as the federal government can go in enforcing secrecy, short of prosecuting for espionage. In this country, there has never been an Official Secrets Act of the British sort, making it a crime to release national security information without authorization. By contrast, American police chase spies under espionage statutes but rarely play any role in investigating the less dramatic cases of mishandled secrets. Thus, with only limited means of legal sanction, the American system of protecting critical information relies heavily upon techniques of prevention. Procedures are designed to make it rare that secrets are mishandled in the first place.

Some experts recommend business practices that parallel the government clearance process. It is sometimes recommended that employers compile a list of trade secrets to which a prospective employee could have access and the potential damage to the company of a loss of each. Employees should be evaluated during job interviews in light of such potential damage they could cause the company and their trustworthiness. Most companies cannot carry out the extensive background checks that federal agencies sometimes perform, but it is often prudent to assign or hire an investigator to verify data supplied by the job applicant.

One difference between business and government is the former's greater reliance on employee agreements. Explicit discussion with employees of the risks surrounding trade secrets and their signing of contracts that set out what they can and cannot do with information they learn while working for a company are key elements in impressing a court with the seriousness of an information-protection program.

Physical Security and Document Control

Physical security programs are concerned with the physical aspects of delivering classified information in a secure way to cleared individuals with a need-to-know and keeping it from everyone else.

Classified documents must be stored securely, and guidelines and technology have been developed for doing this. Sometimes specific procedures must be created for transporting sensitive materials. Often, they are not allowed to leave the building in which they are stored; guards must then check individuals thoroughly who leave to make sure that this remains the case. Even when such materials can be removed, guards may require some kind of authorization.

Guards at entrances also monitor who is entering and leaving facilities, and they may require escorts for visitors. They may prevent cameras, tape recorders and other equipment from being brought into facilities. Certain sections of facilities may be off-limits to all but cleared persons; both human and technical means are used to guarantee compliance.

Officials responsible for physical security set up rules and methods for keeping inventories of classified documents, of reproducing such documents and of physically destroying them. Procedures also govern the return of documents to storage when they are not in use. These officials are often responsible for ensuring that individuals attending meetings at a facility are aware of the classification rules in effect and that visits to such meetings by outsiders are monitored.

Security officials prepare written reports of infractions of security procedures and discuss infractions with the violator and his or her supervisor. In many agencies, disciplinary action is administered not by security officials but by a violator's superiors. Agencies generally have written procedures surrounding disciplinary action; these often include ways to appeal actions.

An agency's physical security office can also be a close adjunct to traditional security activities. One former public affairs director at the CIA has described his job there as "damage control" to learn, through carefully cultivated relations with the media, when stories about the CIA were about to appear, so that agency officials could plan a response.

Public affairs offices also seek to provide a good image of the agency they represent by portraying it as soundly managed, acting properly and able to make corrections when problems occur. A good image helps security managers protect critical information in three ways. It helps foster the relationships with reporters that officials may need to carry out damage control. It prevents the kind of journalistic digging that leads to disclosures by making digging seem unnecessary. And it creates a public perception that the agency can successfully address its problems in-house, through its own security people, and that accomplishing this does not require the pressure of press revelations.

The experience of government with physical security and public affairs is directly relevant to the needs of business. While some federal agencies physically protect information with expensive and highly sophisticated equipment which may go beyond the needs of a private company, most of the government's security techniques—the use of guards, restrictions on removing information from facilities, locked storage, central control of significant documents, and so on—probably fall under the courts' conception of the "reasonable measures" companies should use to protect trade secrets.

And a prudent business can use its public affairs office as much as do agencies like the CIA to prevent unwanted press disclosures and to succeed with damage control after they have occurred.

Computer Security

Computer security presents special problems. A computerized data storage system is said to be "trusted" if access to it is controlled. Various levels of trust reflect the extent and nature of limits on access to items within the computer. Some federal computers, such as those at the National Security Agency, are only accessible on-site; they cannot be reached by phone lines or from a remote facility. Those which are not secure in this way are vulnerable to sabotage and theft from off-site.

Largely the same scheme of classification is used when the classified data is stored electronically in a computer as that used for paper documents. A major difference, of course, is in the physical markings, since computer information is not represented on paper. Hardware that contains classified data is labeled as such. So, too, is software, which is sometimes structured to control access based on sensitivity.

Sophisticated software that controls access to computer data is available, both on-site and from off-site, through passwords and other devices. Clever programmers, however, can often develop schemes to get around these barriers, and federal computer security experts try to anticipate such schemes and prevent them from having success.

Many private companies, such as phone companies and credit agencies, must maintain the confidentiality of their computer data bases to protect the rights of clients, and these companies may already be familiar with techniques used by government to keep computer information secure.

As more information becomes computerized, the government's experience with sophisticated techniques to maintain security will be increasingly relevant to the activities of business.

OPSEC and Counterintelligence

This leaves the work of identifying and doing something about unclassified information that may be used by adversaries and the media in order to piece together classified facts. It also leaves the work of identifying and stopping the actual covert operations adversaries use to collect sensitive intelligence. The first is operations security, or OPSEC; the second is counterintelligence.

OPSEC is an outgrowth of the military's experience in Vietnam. To maintain the element of surprise in America's Rolling Thunder air strikes against targets in North Vietnam, the Joint Chiefs of Staff initiated a study to identify indicators that the Vietnamese could exploit for advance warning. A formal office was soon set up to uncover indicators and to develop countermeasures.

After the war, however, the idea was in decline until the Reagan Administration revived it. President Reagan signed an Executive Order in 1988 setting up the interagency OPSEC office and ordering a review of national security programs for the availability of unclassified indicators of sensitive facts.

Concern had been growing in the intelligence community over the ability of novelists like Tom Clancy and a number of journalists to piece together a picture of covert military programs entirely from open sources of information. The presidential directive mandated a five-step process to address this concern.

The first step is identification of critical information about American programs or activities which a competing or adversarial nation might seek out in order to gain an advantage over the United States. Second is the analysis of specific targeting against specific critical information. What are potential adversaries in fact seeking? Third is the analysis of the vulnerability of that critical information, whether through open or illicit sources. The final two steps in this process are assessment of risks of losing the critical information and the application of appropriate countermeasures.

Counterintelligence is the business of locating spies and neutralizing the threats they pose. There are three ways that spies can be handled. Counterintelligence agents can behave as police and treat them as criminals, arresting, prosecuting, and placing them in prison. Or American agents may focus on countermeasures, warning those who work with the spies and to quietly have them removed from positions where they can threaten national security.

Finally, counterintelligence operatives may want the spies, once uncovered, to remain in place and to continue their espionage, even while trying to reduce the damage they may cause. This strategy may involve surveillance to find out who they work for and who their contacts are. It might also involve attempts to "turn" them, to convince them to become double-agents against their former masters.

Some business consultants think it may be prudent for companies to employ methods like OPSEC and perhaps even counterintelligence techniques. Unlike the entirely defensive measures discussed earlier, both OPSEC and counterintelligence are pro-active; their practitioners assume the worst about the vulnerability of U.S. institutions and about the effectiveness of preventive measures of information protection. They assume national security has been breached and intend to locate specific breaches. Some say that the current business environment warrants similar attitudes.

The New National Industrial Security Program

President Bush approved a landmark industry-government report outlining the new National Industrial Security Program (NISP) in January, 1992, setting the way for a new executive order and security manual that will streamline inefficient policies for protecting classified information.

In a memorandum to Defense Secretary Dick Cheney, the president said he was "especially pleased" with plans to fully implement the new industrial security program by 1995. "The government-industry task force you established has made considerable progress toward development of a single, coherent, and integrated program," the president states.

The president called the NISP a "vital program which will provide cost effective and secure development and delivery of systems essential to our national security."

The NISP report was presented to the White House in October, 1991, by Donald J. Atwood, deputy defense secretary, Adm. James D. Watkins, secretary of energy, and Richard J. Kerr, at the time acting director of central intelligence.

The report was put together over eight months by a joint government-industry task force that has been examining ways to develop a single integrated, cohesive, industrial security program to protect classified information. The NISP is also needed "to preserve our economic interests and position of technological leadership," the report says.

The program is a unique effort of cooperation among government and the defense industry, which has been complaining for years that security standards for personnel, facilities and information have been plagued by problems that end up being extremely costly.

Nina Stewart, co-chair of the NISP Steering Committee, said defense industry leaders, particularly those in the Aerospace Industries Association, were instrumental in pressing the government to take action on industrial security problems.

"You can't look at the system without seeing that there is an awful lot of duplication out there that could be fixed," Stewart said in an interview. The former executive director of the President's Foreign Intelligence Advisory Board, Stewart was recently named deputy assistant defense secretary for counterintelligence and security countermeasures, a new post.

Key to implementing the new NISP is the signing of an Executive Order outlining the revised industrial security program. The E.O., the legal authority for the program, has been drafted and is "in the coordination phase," Steward said. Final approval, is expected in the summer of 1992.

A key factor pressing the program forward is the recognition that defense programs must operate in a climate of vastly decreasing resources, Stewart said. As a result, business and government both need more cost effective industrial security procedures, she said.

"I believe this program will more than pay for itself," Stewart said.

Some organizations may suffer costs increases at the start of implementing new program because their security standards may have been below acceptable levels, she said. "But there will be other organizations that will see net savings increase almost immediately and then over the long term, once we have a more efficient system, it can't help but save significant amounts," Stewart said.

According to Stewart, the major milestones for implementing the new industrial security program this year will be the completion of a new or revised executive order, and the publication of a manual outlining common standards for security, applicable to both government and industry.

Don Fuqua, president of the Aerospace Industries Association, which played a key role in developing the NISP, said industry has pressed for the reforms after decades of confusing, duplicative and overlapping procedures.

"Something should have been done about it a long time ago," Fuqua said in an interview. "But nobody ever got around to it." He said the amount of money that could be saved by both industry and government from the NISP, by some estimates, could be as much as $3 billion.

The task in fixing industrial security problems was enormous, given the bureaucratic complexity of existing procedures and enormous variations in each agency's requirements.

Fuqua also stressed that the program will improve security and save money at a time of tight budgets, when business is looking for ways to eliminate duplication.

The new program will establish a NISP advisory committee, made up of representatives of government security and intelligence agencies, to handle disputes between agencies on implementing the NISP procedures.

The NISP will also integrate existing databases for personnel security investigations, clearances and access determinations to improve efficiency and eliminate overlap. A new method of receiving, analyzing and distributing threat data will also be established.

"The NISP. . . proposes an industrial security program that protects classified information with reasonable standards in response to the threat, vulnerability and value of the asset," the report states. "It allows the imposition of some supplemental standards or protection techniques as required to protect information of particular sensitivity, to meet intensified threats, or mitigate specific vulnerabilities. The approach meets the demands of change."

Business Becoming More Security-Conscious

Some government officials see trends that will make the federal experience in information security even more relevant to the private sector in the years to come. Since World War II, many innovations in high technology have emanated from Pentagon-sponsored research projects in private industry and at U.S. universities. Many American innovations in computers and communications came about this way.

Because of government sponsorship and their relevance to national security, these projects would often be carried out under a thick veil of national security classification, guaranteeing a long U.S. lead over rivals.

Beginning even before the end of the Cold War, however, the Pentagon has been extricating itself financially from much of this kind of research. It has become more and more the province of private industry alone. The shroud of national security has been lifted. The protections of classification and of the federal information security system have been removed.

At the same time, the business environment has become more competitive. International military tensions have been reduced with the breakup of the Soviet Union, but international economic tensions have increased. The KGB has begun to target economic secrets, but in this arena it follows other foreign intelligence agencies operating against U.S. firms, some operated by so-called "friendly" countries.

Domestically, the competition has grown fiercer as America's share of the pie has become smaller in some sectors. More books appear on business intelligence collection; the subject has even made its way into business schools.

American companies are unprepared for these developments. They have not been forced by war and cold war to take threats to information security as seriously as have their counterparts in the national security bureaucracy. The business environment is only metaphorically warlike and certainly does not command the same emotion or commitment.

Even Pentagon contractors who have security offices to handle matters related to classified projects have not always applied the same resources to protecting their own proprietary business information but were content to depend upon the government security umbrella.

Two things may change this. For one thing, the end of military competition with the Soviet Union has caused the national security bureaucracy to seek out new missions. One that is being pushed hard is the collection of intelligence and counterintelligence in business related areas. The CIA, the NSA and the FBI hope to be working more with private American companies, ferreting out both domestic and international threats.

At the same time, this new mission will not be enough to halt cutbacks in the military and the defense industry. These reductions will result in the retirement of many security managers from government and from defense companies. As they seek employment elsewhere, it is likely that their experience will increasingly filter through to the private sector. With them, they may bring new methods and a new perspective to the job of protecting business secrets.

Chapter 12:

Establishing a Corporate Proprietary Information Protection Program

"We will survive and remain competitive by continuing to stay on the cutting edge of technological developments. We must make sure that our technology is not knowingly or unknowingly stolen by our international competitors."

— James Riesback, Executive Vice President, Corning, Inc.

Corporate America has moved swiftly in recent years to adopt computer systems to store and process an astounding diversity of information ranging from personnel records to new product marketing plans. In that process, many companies have come to recognize that information itself — and not only the computers and other systems that house it — is a strategic and competitive tool.

At the same time, top executives at many major corporations now also recognize that should company information fall into the wrong hands, the result may lead to lawsuits for failing to protect the privacy of company data, missed marketing opportunities or even more disastrous consequences.

A few years ago, for example, at the U.S. Department of Energy's Rocky Flats nuclear weapons plant in Colorado, information systems staffers flouted security measures and stored critical data on nuclear weapons on computer systems that were extremely easy to access via telephone from the outside. Not surprising, DoE officials refused to comment on the episode when it came to light in late 1991, but it is easy to imagine what the potential consequences of this security lapse might have been.

It is readily apparent that organizations — in business and government — that rely on information systems must adopt policies to treat information as an asset and to implement procedures to safeguard it.

As noted, information is an asset — one that organizations seldom properly value until the asset is violated, says one security expert. Information, whether it describes national defense resources, individual health or financial records, automated banking and funds transfer data, or corporate finances, manufacturing processes and marketing strategies, is vital to the ongoing work of an organization, notes Don Gangemi, director of secure systems at Wang Laboratories, Inc.

Information Classification

There are four generally accepted classifications of information: Secret, Confidential, Private and Unclassified. These classifications are defined as follows:

Secret: This classification is applied to an organization's most sensitive business information which is intended to be for use within the organization. Unauthorized release of this information would be severely detrimental to the company's plans and future, its stockholders and its relationship with customers or suppliers.

Confidential: This classification is applied to an organization's less sensitive business information which is intended to be for use within the organization. Unauthorized release of this information also would be detrimental to the company's plans and future, its stockholders and its relationship with customers or suppliers.

Private: This classification is applied to an organization's personal information for use within the organization. Unauthorized release of this information would have an adverse and serious impact on the organization or its employees.

Unclassified: This classification is applied to all other information that does not fit within the above categories. It is intended for use within an organization but its unforeseen release would not have a negative impact on the well-being of the organization or its employees. Some organizations include a subset of this classification called *public* that is applied to information specifically intended to be released to the public.

Like any other asset, information is owned. Ownership carries with it certain rights and responsibilities, according to Gangemi. The owner of a body of information is responsible for exercising property rights over that information. These rights include:

- Designating who can and cannot access the information.

- Determining what kind of access is allowed (e.g., some individuals may be allowed only to read the information; others to read, change and even dispose of it).

- Protecting the information from unauthorized or inadvertent access by taking advantage of available methods to secure it.

Information Costs Versus Risks

Security expert Gangemi notes that any organization that is evaluating its information assets and considering whether and how to protect these assets must answer three important questions:

How important is the information? There are many different types of information ranging from national defense information describing military resources to corporate records showing projected profits and losses, strategic business and marketing plans, etc.

What is the cost of securing the information? There are many different costs. These include determining whether new equipment must be purchased; whether the security controls will hamper the work of the employees who must use it daily; and whether it will be possible to reconstruct information that is lost.

How vulnerable is the information? Some information may be of great value to a company but of no benefit to anyone outside of the organization. Other information may be of great interest but simply so inaccessible that it may not pay to protect it beyond justifiable security methods.

Protection of Sensitive Information

An effective information security program is an elegant blend of physical, personnel, and communications protective measures. In general, complete programs of data protection include the following elements at a minimum:

- ❑ Policy and procedural statements on the recognition, classification, and handling of sensitive information.

- ❑ Pre-employment screening and employee review procedures to determine whether prospective and current employees are apt to exploit information that is placed in their care.

- ❑ Nondisclosure agreements from employees, in which they acknowledge their fiduciary responsibility to protect information and the consequences of their failure to do so.

- ❑ The signing of noncompetitive agreements by employees who are at risk of divulging sensitive or proprietary information to outsiders should they decide to leave the company.

❑ The implementation of standard physical security measures such as access controls, identification badges and procedures, secured storage containers, regulated copying facilities, controlled trash disposal, and restrictions on use of computer media to minimize the probability that unauthorized persons will gain access to sensitive data on or off the premises.

❑ Security awareness programs that instruct employees on how to handle sensitive information and their responsibilities in assuring that the information in their care is properly protected according to the company's policies and procedures.

Threats to Information

More information is lost as a result of errors or inadvertent admission by employees than by hackers, industrial spies or espionage agents, according to many security professionals. Information can be accidentally given out to competitors and others by marketing people giving sales presentations, purchasing agents at trade shows and public relations professionals distributing news releases to the media.

"The primary threat is due to negligence and unintentional release of information," says the security chief at one large American corporation. "I don't see a lot of people in trench coats trying to sneak into our building by tunneling a hole under the fence to steal information.

"There are more and more companies out there starting to understand the value of information. I think it's evidenced by the very rapid growth of the Society of Competitive Intelligence Professionals. There are a lot of companies who have people in positions to gather competitive intelligence.

"They're not out there acting as spies and getting people intoxicated in bars, trying to get information out of them, but in fact they're always out there with their eyes and ears open and they're looking. If our employees are not careful with what they're giving out, they end up allowing information to get out that should not be made public where competitors pick up on it."

The governing rule for direct access to information is need-to-know. If employees don't need-to-know, they should not have access. That rule applies to virtually all corporate information, whether it is considered sensitive or not. However, even the information that is not considered sensitive should be safeguarded, if only to avoid the inconvenience of its loss or corruption.

A peripheral benefit of the need-to-know rule is that if data is damaged, it narrows the field of authorized users. If the damage results from user error, there is an opportunity to train the offending user so the error is not repeated. Knowing who the valid users are makes it possible for the security professional to eliminate them as the damage's source and to look for an intruder or other offender.

Outsider Threats to Information

There are numerous — perhaps hundreds — of ways that information may be acquired by outsiders bent on probing a company's secrets. The following list summarizes only a few of them and is not meant to be comprehensive. Use these examples as a starting point to assess your company's vulnerabilities:

- Electronic eavesdropping. All electronic equipment emits electromagnetic radiation that can be intercepted using electronic gear that can be assembled from parts purchased at a Radio Shack.

- Hardware and software loopholes. Computer equipment and programs pose several challenges to security professionals. Computer networks, which are proliferating rapidly, allow hackers and others to surreptitiously enter a company's database and download information. Particularly savvy hackers can leave behind loopholes in software that allow them to return at will.

- Taps and bugs. Telephones and other communication lines can be tapped to siphon off information. Similarly, information transmitted via fax machines can be intercepted.

Case Study: Monsanto Company Security Guidelines and Policies

Monsanto Company, based in St. Louis, Mo., has developed a comprehensive approach to establishing computer security guidelines and procedures to classify and protect proprietary company information. The following material was provided by Genevieve M. Burns, manager, data security, in the Monsanto Corporate Management Information Systems Department.

The company's first line of defense against the unwanted disclosure of company information and secrets is its information protection and classification policy:

An information protection policy was developed by the corporate security department and issued throughout the company with the support of senior management of each organization. The worldwide dissemination of this policy ensures all company employees are aware of the policy and its contents.

Information assets are defined as the spoken word, hand-written materials, typed or printed materials, computer-generated reports and computer-stored data. In addition to the business reasons for the protection of information assets, it is required by the courts to show due diligence in the protection of those assets if legal proceedings should become necessary. This policy sets the stage for the classification of information and the concept that all information does not require classification with its implied protection.

Two types of classified or restricted information are defined:

Company Confidential

This is information that, if disclosed outside of a need-to-know or legal context, could result in substantial harm to the company. Examples include research and development information, manufacturing information, financial forecasts, marketing plans, patents and trade secrets, sales information and cost data.

Company Private

This category applies to personnel information that, if disclosed outside of a need-to-know or legal context, could be seriously detrimental to individual employees or the company. This includes information covered by the government's privacy laws. Examples include employee medical records, personal history statements, personnel folders, performance reviews, salaries of individuals and other information of a personal nature provided to the company as a requirement of employment.

The policy requires that the originator of proprietary information ensure it is properly classified. It requires all printed information, including that displayed on a computer to be labeled on each page or screen to facilitate proper handling of the material. It requires the originator of the material, the employee responsible for the material or individual responsible for profit and loss in the program area, to authorize any reproduction of Company Confidential or Company Private information. The issues of access-dissemination, disclosure to outside parties, transmittal and disposal-destruction are also covered.

Marking

Documents and other media such as pictorial or electronic-computer materials shall carry the appropriate marking if these media contain information that fits the guidelines for protection. The purpose of marking is to facilitate proper handling of the document. The legend Company Confidential or Company Private shall be placed on each page of the document containing classified information.

Valuing data

It is just as important to know what data to protect as how to protect it. It is up to each of us to be aware of the degree of protection we must apply to the data we process. The following defines data that must be protected from an information protection policy and/or control and recovery perspective.

INFORMATION PROTECTION POLICY

Definition

Example

Company Confidential data

Data which, if disclosed to individuals other than those with a specific need-to-know, would result in substantial harm to the company.

Financial results
Marketing strategies
Research data
Company plans
Trade secrets

Company Private data

Data of a personal nature, which, if disclosed to individuals other than those with a specific need-to-know, would be seriously detrimental to individual employees or the company. This also applies to data covered by government privacy laws.

Employee medical data
Personnel history data
Salary and payroll data

Sensitive data Data that, if used or modified inappropriately, could result in fraud, embezzlement, misappropriation, loss, or misrepresentation of assets.	Accounts payable data Salary and payroll data Receivables data Inventory data
Critical data Data without which normal business operations would be significantly disrupted or seriously impaired	Order handling data Inventory data Billing data Freight schedules

A Special Case: Desktop Computer Security Guidelines

Personal computers and workstations store and process more information than ever thought possible only a few years ago. As a result, the possibility of destroying massive amounts of information and programs is correspondingly greater. A computer virus, for example, can wipe out an entire data base in the about the same time it takes to read this sentence.

Desktop computer systems are being installed in all corners of corporate offices and stitched together in intricate networks that span the globe. It becomes increasingly difficult to protect systems and the number of entry points into a company's computers are multiplying.

Many of the users are untrained about computer security and may not have the same attitude about protecting company secrets as staffers in the data center. Although mistakes continue to be the most common way to lose data, threats are becoming more common, in relationship with the rapid growth in the number of computer-literate people around the world.

Thus, security professionals believe that personal computer security requires specialized guidelines.

At Monsanto, microcomputer security is addressed from two perspectives:

◆ Data Protection: The confidentiality of Monsanto data, processed on a microcomputer or associated peripherals must be maintained.

◆ Equipment Protection: Safeguards must be provided, on a cost-justified basis, for microcomputers and associated peripherals to minimize potential loss due to power surges, theft, malicious acts or accidental destruction.

Keys to Responsibility

The management of each organization that uses microcomputers is responsible for the communication and enforcement of this policy.

Users are responsible for the protection of their data on microcomputers and the protection of the equipment.

Each microcomputer will have a designated person responsible for its management.

The MIS function is responsible for providing training, consulting, and implementation support on the proper use and control of microcomputer equipment and associated data.

Keys to Data Protection

Data classified under the information protection policy as Company Confidential or Company Private will be protected against unauthorized disclosure as follows:

- If stored on removable data storage, the storage media must be secured when not in use.

- If stored on non-removable storage media, the data must be protected with systems that reasonably control who may access the data.

From a control perspective, sensitive data must be protected against unauthorized changes. From a recovery perspective, critical data must be backed up and the backup copy stored in a secure place remote from the workstation.

Keys to Protecting Equipment

Microcomputers and associated peripherals that fall into the following categories must be stored in a secure area or protected by anti-theft mechanisms recommended by the MIS function:

- Difficult to replace and if stolen would cause a significant disruption in work flow.

- Expensive to replace.

- Contains Company Confidential or Company Private data.

Sample: A Brief Information Security Policy Statement

Noted computer security consultant, Charles Cresson Wood, has published a comprehensive set of information security policies in a book entitled: *Information Security Policies Made Easy*.

This book contains more than 100 pages of useful and timely information that can be used to create, modify and enhance corporate information procedures, including developing a plan to classify and protect company information.

Registered purchasers of the book may copy and republish information for use in creating materials for in-house policy statements. The entire book is also available on floppy diskette to help speed that process. Contact Baseline Software, P.O. Box 1219, Sausalito, Calif. 94966; tel: (415)332-7763 for more information.

The following sample of a brief information security policy statement appears in Wood's book:

Information and information systems are critical and important to Company X assets. Without reliable information and information systems, Company X would quickly go out of business. Accordingly, Company X management has a fiduciary duty to preserve, increase, and account for Company X information and information systems.

This means that Company X management must take appropriate steps to ensure that information and information systems are properly protected from a variety of threats such as error, fraud, embezzlement, sabotage, terrorism, extortion, industrial espionage, privacy violation, and natural disaster.

Company X information must be protected in a manner commensurate with its sensitivity, value, and criticality. Security measures must be employed regardless of the media on which information is stored (paper, overhead transparency, computer bits, etc.), the systems which process it (microcomputers, mainframes, voice mail systems, etc.), or the methods by which it is moved (electronic mail, face-to-face conversation, etc.). Such protection includes restricting access to information based on the need-to-know.

Management must devote sufficient time and resources to ensure that information is properly protected. Company X management must additionally make sure that information and information systems are protected in a manner that is at least as secure as other organizations in the same industry handling the same type of information. To achieve this objective, annual reviews of the risks to Company X information and information systems must be conducted. Similarly, whenever a major security incident indicates that the security of information or information systems is insufficient, management must take remedial action to reduce Company X's exposure. Annual reports reflecting Company X's information security status and progress must also be prepared and submitted to the president/CEO.

Decision-making within Company X is also critically dependent on information and information systems. Management must make reasonable efforts to ensure that all Company X information is accurate, timely, relevant, and complete.

So that it may consider the reliability of information, management must be notified of these and other information attributes. Attention to and fine-tuning of information attributes is expected to provide Company X with a competitive advantage.

All employees, consultants, and contractors must be provided with sufficient training and supporting reference materials to allow them to properly protect and otherwise manage Company X information assets.

Training materials should communicate that information security is an important part of Company X's business, and must be viewed like other on-going business functions such as accounting and marketing.

Guidance, direction, and authority for information security activities is centralized for the entire organization in the Information Security Department.

The Information Security Department is responsible for establishing and maintaining organization-wide information security policies, standards, guidelines, and procedures.

Promoting Computer Security Awareness

Somewhere between 50 to 70% of all security problems are due to accidents and employees unaware they are breaking rules, says Dennis Flanders, of The

Boeing Company. Computer security guidelines and policies must be continually reinforced with an awareness program if they are to be effective, according to several security experts.

The following is a list of tools in use by AT&T Bell Laboratories, Metropolitan Life and several other corporations that are useful in waging a campaign to foster adherence to security procedures:

Security Awareness Campaign Tools:

Talks — Nothing will ever take the place of face-to-face talks with employees. They present opportunities to make suggestions that are specific to the group or department; handle questions as soon as they arise; gauge the attitudes and familiarity with protecting corporate assets and information systems.

Videos — Today's employee has been raised on television, thus it is not surprising that videos on security topics are an effective means of communicating security awareness to employees. A discussion and handouts following the session will help reinforce the security message.

Newsletters — Company newsletters can be an invaluable way of regularly promoting security awareness. Write articles on a variety of topics. Keep them brief and to the point.

Posters — Develop a security theme and support it with a series of posters that stand out from others that may be posted in your company. Keep the messages simple and direct; use a variety of approaches, from the serious to the humorous.

Brochures and Booklets — A simple booklet or brochure can be used to reinforce the security message or serve as a reminder to employees. Keep them easy to read and avoid using an overly serious tone.

Trinkets — Everyone loves a freebie. Post-it notes, pens, mouse pads, stickers and the like also spread the security message. If carefully chosen, the trinket will be both handy and readily in sight.

Awards — An award for fostering security or for implementing innovative security techniques is a positive approach to awareness. Make them valuable by giving them only when they are truly deserved.

Several companies mix and match the above campaign tools according to the audience's size and sophistication. Here is one approach used at AT&T Bell Laboratories that can be easily applied to a variety of organizations:

First, determine who is the audience?

- Executive

- Management

- Clerical

- Technical background

Sample security program targets:

- small/single site

  — administrator presentation, video, handouts

  — follow-up with posters and articles; periodicals, periodic topic booklets

- numerous sites

  — central control

  — coordinator's presentation, video, handouts

  — follow up with posters and articles; periodicals, periodic topic booklets

- large decentralized organization

  — headquarters-developed package, local management letter, standard approach, stand-alone videos

  — follow up with sample packages, ordering capability, headquarters support

Computer Security Awareness Day

Each year, on December 2, the Association for Computing Machinery (ACM), among other groups, sponsors a Computer Security Awareness Day to publicize the potential dangers of inadequate computer security procedures and policies. The following is a list of 50 ways to participate in Computer Security Awareness Day (we added a few more for good measure):

1. Display computer security posters

2. Present computer security briefings

3. Change passwords

4. Present a computer security video, film or slide show

5.   Check for computer viruses

6.   Protect against static electricity

7.   Modify the log-on message on the computer system to notify users that Computer Security Day is December 2nd.

8.   Vacuum the computer and the immediate area

9.   Clean the heads on disk drives and tape back-up systems

10. Back up data

11. Delete unneeded files

13. Demonstrate computer security software

14. Publicize existing computer security policies

15. Issue new computer security guidelines

16. Declare an amnesty day for computer security violators who wish to reform

17. Announce Computer Security Day in the company newsletter

18. Examine the audit files on computers

19. Verify that the welcome message normally used on computers is appropriate for the organization

20. Put write-protect tabs on diskettes that are not supposed to be written to

21. Take the write-protect rings out of the tapes in the library

22. Verify the inventory of computer applications

23. Verify the inventory of computer utilities and packaged software

24. Verify the inventory of computer hardware

25. Verify the inventory of computer networks

26. Inspect and install power protection equipment as appropriate

27. Inspect or install fire and smoke detectors and suppression equipment in computer areas

28. Eliminate dust from computer areas, including chalk dust

29. Provide disk and water covers for personal and larger computers

30. Post "No drinking, eating and smoking" signs in computer areas

31. Develop or review the recovery plan for all computers

32. Verify that passwords are not posted

33. Verify that back-up power and air conditioning exists to support computer operations

34. Have a mini-training session to provide all computer users with a basic understanding of computer security.

35. Verify that all source codes are protected from unauthorized changes

36.   Verify that each computer has its own trouble log and that it is being used

37.   Verify that appropriate offsite storage exists and is being used

38.   Remove all unnecessary items such as extra supplies, coat racks and printouts from the computer room

39.   Select a system on which to perform a risk analysis

40.   Begin planning next year's Computer Security Day

41.   Change FORMAT command in MS-DOS to avoid accidentally formatting disk drives

42.   Protect the computer on the store-and-forward phone system

43.   Hold a discussion about ethics with computer users

44.   Volunteer to speak at a local computer club

45.   Collect Computer Security Day memorabilia to trade with others

46.   Register and pay for all shareware used regularly

47.   Apply all security-related patches to the operating system

49.   Help novice users back up their files this week

50.   Attend an ACM Computer Security Day Seminar

To those we add a few more:

51.   Develop a policy that forbids employees from using diskettes brought from home in company computers

52.   Install antivirus software on PCs and scan all new programs before they are installed

53.   Change voice-mail passwords

Safeguarding the Company's Bottom Line

The information revolution has of necessity spawned the need for information responsibility. Part of that responsibility is the prioritization of information, determining which information should be categorized as proprietary.

Increasingly, companies are discovering the need to protect proprietary information, and the need to classify proprietary information according to its value as a corporate asset. Information security, companies are learning, is in every employee's interest.

The cost of information protection isn't negligible, but the old maxim applies here: you get what you pay for. Rest assured, the cost of not protecting information is higher. Never before in American economic history has industrial and technological competition proved to be as vital, as fierce, as expensive or as sophisticated. Effective information security isn't just the key to increased profits, it's the key to economic survival.

Conclusion

C orporate America, perhaps more than any other institution in the world, has proven that knowledge is indeed power. Information — how it's gathered, stored, protected and distributed — has become a competitive weapon, a strategic tool and even a currency of business. Ironically, in the process of acquiring information technology, some companies are putting their proprietary information at risk in ways never before realized.

As U.S. companies battle for market share in an increasingly competitive world market, the risks of their sensitive information being stolen or acquired legally by competitive intelligence gatherers, professional electronic eavesdroppers, outlaw hackers and others can only increase.

The preceding chapters build the case for senior managers and executives to take the threat of economic espionage seriously and assess their company's exposure to information theft or loss. Those organizations requiring a more detailed auditing of corporate information and communications systems, should seek out the services of a security professional.

The future of corporate America's success in the highly competitive global economy that we no longer dominate, will be increasingly defined by how well we protect our sensitive technologies and proprietary business information assets.

Our nation's stake in the effectiveness of protecting information is considerable and will loom even larger as we approach the 21st century.